GRATITUDE VIBEZ

Dr Gratitude

This is the positive book of Dr. Gratitude—author, speaker, and advocate for living with purpose and positivity. Here, you'll find my journey, offerings, inspiration, and powerful insights on gratitude, energy, and transformation.

GRATITUDE VIBEZ

The Gratitude Method Publishing House

© 2025 by Alicia Ann Wade

All Rights Reserved

All rights reserved. No part of this book may be used or reproduced in any form whatsoever without written permission except in the case of brief quotations in critical articles or reviews.

DISCLAIMER
Because of the dynamic nature of the Internet, any web addresses or links contained in this book may have changed since publication and may no longer be valid. The views expressed in this work are solely those of the author and do not necessarily reflect the views of the publisher, and the publisher hereby disclaims any responsibility for them. The author of this book does no dispense medical advice or prescribe the use of any technique as a form of treatment for physical, emotional, or medical problems without the advice of a physician, either directly or indirectly. The intent of the author is only to offer information of a general nature to help you in your quest for emotional and spiritual well-being. In the event you use any of the information in this book for yourself, which is your constitutional right, the author and the publisher assume no responsibility for your actions.

For more information, or to book an event, contact :

info@thegratitudemethod.com

http://wwwthegratitudemethod.com

Thank you to:
Photographer: Charlotte Marshall The Branding Bar Studio Sunshine Coast
Make up: Melinda Dee Make Up Artistry
Studio: Frank X Studio Sunshine Coast

Printed by The Gratitude Method TM

Printed in the Australia
Available from Website and other retail outlets
First Printing Edition, 2025

Welcome to Gratitude Vibez! As you read through these pages, you're stepping into something special—an opportunity to see yourself, your life, and the world around you in a whole new light.

This isn't just a book; it's a chance to open your heart, lift your spirit, and let gratitude guide you to more joy and abundance. There will be moments to reflect, smile, and maybe even discover things you didn't expect.

Remember, gratitude has a way of showing up just when you need it most. Stay open, stay curious, and trust the journey. Whether you're here to bring a dream to life or simply find more peace, I'm cheering you on every step of the way.

Wishing you joy, magic, and endless good vibes!

With Gratitude,

Dr. Gratitude
Alicia Wade

FROM THE AUTHOR

CONTENTS

1
Gratitude 101: Your Superpower Unleashed
- Discover Your Inner Gratitude Guru 1
- The Science of Sparkles 5
- Gratitude Check-In 7

2
Vibez Don't Lie: Understanding Energy Magic
- Energy 101 with a Twist 13
- High Vibes Only 15
- Vibe-O-Metre 20

3
From Lack to Lavish: Flipping the Abundance Switch
- Ditch the Scarcity Syndrome 27
- Activate Abundance Mode 28
- Gratitude Game Plan 31

4
Gratitude, Unplugged: Creating Your Personal Practice
- Build Your Gratitude Groove 37
- The Art of Gratitude Journaling 39
- Gratitude on the Go 43

5
The Manifestation Frequency: Tuning into the Good Life
- Manifesting 101: 49
- Visualise, Gratify, Manifest 51
- Manifestation Magic Tricks 53

6
Clearing the Vibe Blockers: Say Bye-Bye to Energy Drains
- What's Blocking Your Shine? 61
- Vibe Detox 65
- Forgive and Fly Free 69

7
Gratitude Love Fest: Supercharge Your Relationships
- Gratitude in Action 75
- The Gratitude Love Language 78
- Healing with Heart 83

8
Gratitude Glow-Up: How Thankfulness Heals and Thrills

- Feel-Good Gratitude 89
- The Gratitude Spa Day 92
- Gratitude + Health Hacks 98

9
Gratitude Genie: Wish, Believe, Receive

- Setting Grateful Intentions 109
- The Gratitude Genie Formula 112
- Real-Life Magic Stories 115

10
Living in the Gratitude Groove: Make It a Lifestyle

- The Gratitude Lifestyle 122
- Staying High on the Vibe Train 125
- The Gratitude Vision 128

11
Conclusion

- Your Gratitude Journey 136
- A Final Sprinkle of Magic 141

CONTENTS

YOUR POWER ISN'T HIDDEN—IT'S IN EVERY MOMENT YOU CHOOSE TO SEE THE GOOD AND LET IT GROW

Gratitude 101: Your Superpower Unleashed

CHAPTER 1

Discover Your Inner Gratitude Guru
Let's Begin...

Welcome to the start of something seriously magical—your journey to becoming a Gratitude Guru! You might be wondering, "What on earth is a Gratitude Guru?" Well, it's you, my friend! That's right. By the end of this chapter, you'll see just how powerful you are when you tap into the incredible force of gratitude. But before we dive into this superpower, let's clear up what a Gratitude Guru actually is.

A Gratitude Guru isn't a mystical figure perched on a mountain, dispensing pearls of wisdom (although that does sound pretty cool). A Gratitude Guru is simply someone who has mastered the art of appreciating life in all its glory—the good, the bad, and the in-between. It's about living with an open heart, seeing the beauty in the mundane, and using gratitude as a tool to transform your life from the inside out. And guess what? That someone is you!

Now, let's get to the heart of the matter: gratitude itself. You've probably heard the word a million times—on social media, in self-help books, maybe even from your well-meaning friends or family. But have you ever stopped to think about what it really means?

Gratitude isn't just about saying "thank you" when someone holds the door open for you (though that's a good start!). It's so much more. It's about feeling a deep sense of appreciation for all the good things in your life, big or small. Think of gratitude as a lens through which you view the world. Imagine putting on a pair of magical glasses that suddenly make everything look brighter, clearer, and more beautiful. That's what gratitude does for your soul.

Here's the deal: Gratitude is a superpower, and the best part is, you already have it! You don't need to be bitten by a radioactive spider or born on another planet to access it. You don't need to attend a secret school of gratitude or learn from a master (though, if that existed, it would be amazing). All you have to do is start noticing the good stuff around you— and trust me, there's plenty of it.

Gratitude doesn't always have to be about the big, life-changing events. Sure, it's easy to be thankful when you land your dream job, find the love of your life, or go on that vacation you've been dreaming of for years. But the real magic of gratitude lies in the small stuff —the everyday moments that we often overlook.

Think about the feeling of warm sunlight on your face after days of rain, the smell of your favourite coffee brewing in the morning, or the way your pet greets you with boundless enthusiasm after a long day. These are the little sparks of joy that, when noticed and appreciated, can fill your life with a constant stream of positivity.

As a Gratitude Guru, your mission is to tune into these moments. It's about shifting your focus from what's wrong or missing in your life to what's right and abundant. The more you practice this, the more natural it becomes, until one day you realise that your life is overflowing with things to be grateful for—even on the tough days.

Here's where the real power of gratitude comes into play. Gratitude isn't just about feeling good in the moment—it's a mindset, a way of seeing the world that can completely shift your perspective. When you practice gratitude consistently, you start to notice that your thoughts, feelings, and even your actions begin to change.

Gratitude IS Your Secret Superpower

Suddenly, challenges don't seem as daunting because you've trained your mind to find the silver lining. Annoyances and setbacks become opportunities to learn and grow. Even in the midst of chaos, you can find calm by focusing on what you're thankful for. This isn't about ignoring life's difficulties; it's about choosing to focus on what's working, rather than what's not.

Gratitude turns what we have into enough. It shifts our focus from lack to abundance, from fear to love, from frustration to peace. And that, my friend, is the true power of being a Gratitude Guru.

So, how do you unlock this superpower and start living like a Gratitude Guru? It's simpler than you might think. It all starts with awareness—just paying attention to the good things that happen throughout your day.

You don't need to make grand gestures or have life-changing epiphanies to experience the benefits of gratitude. Start small. Maybe it's writing down three things you're grateful for each morning or taking a moment at the end of the day to reflect on what went well. The key is consistency. The more you practice gratitude, the more it becomes a part of who you are.

Think of it like building a muscle. At first, it might feel a little awkward or forced, but with time and practice, it becomes stronger, and soon enough, it becomes second nature. Your gratitude muscle will help you lift yourself out of negativity, stress, and fear, and carry you into a space of positivity, resilience, and joy.

YOUR JOURNEY BEGINS

Congratulations! You've just taken the first step on your journey to becoming a Gratitude Guru. As you continue through this chapter, and indeed this book, you'll discover more ways to harness the power of gratitude in your everyday life. You'll learn how to shift your mindset, raise your vibration, and start attracting more of what you want into your life.

But for now, just take a moment to appreciate where you are. You've opened yourself up to a new way of thinking and living. And that, my friend, is something to be truly grateful for.

So, are you ready to embrace your inner Gratitude Guru? The journey ahead is filled with discoveries, joy, and, of course, a whole lot of gratitude.

Let's Get Started

THE SCIENCE OF SPARKLES

GRATITUDE LIGHTS UP YOUR SOUL LIKE FIREWORKS—SET IT OFF, AND WATCH YOUR WORLD GLOW

Okay, now let's dive into some fun science. Did you know that when you feel grateful, your brain actually lights up like a Christmas tree? Seriously, it's true! It turns out that your brain loves gratitude, and when you practice it regularly, it's like giving your mind and body a little high-five. But how does this actually work?

Here's the scoop: when you experience feelings of gratitude, your brain releases a cocktail of feel-good chemicals—dopamine and serotonin being the headliners. Dopamine is often called the "reward" chemical because it makes you feel all warm and fuzzy inside, giving you that sweet sense of satisfaction. Serotonin, on the other hand, is the "happy" chemical, helping to regulate your mood and keep anxiety and depression at bay. Together, these chemicals create a happiness boost that can turn even an average day into a pretty great one.

But that's not all. When you practice gratitude regularly, your brain actually starts to rewire itself. Yep, you read that right—your brain can literally change shape and function thanks to gratitude. This is called neuroplasticity, and it's the brain's ability to reorganise itself by forming new neural connections. Think of it like updating the software on your phone. Gratitude upgrades your brain's operating system, making it more efficient at noticing and appreciating the positive things in life.

So, what does all this mean for you? For starters, practicing gratitude doesn't just make you feel good in the moment—it has long-term benefits that can transform your overall well-being. Studies have shown that people who regularly practice gratitude have better mental health, less stress, and even stronger immune systems. They're also more resilient, meaning they're better equipped to handle life's inevitable ups and downs.

In fact, one study found that people who kept a gratitude journal for just three weeks reported higher levels of happiness and optimism—and these effects lasted for months afterward. It's like a ripple effect of positivity that keeps spreading long after you've written down what you're thankful for.

And here's where the real magic happens: the more you practice gratitude, the easier it becomes to find things to be grateful for. It's like training your brain to search for sparkles in every situation. Even on a tough day, you'll start to notice those little bright spots—like the stranger who smiled at you, or the cozy feeling of your favorite sweater. It's those small moments of joy that, when added together, create a life that's positively sparkling.

So, think of gratitude as the sparkles you add to your day. Every time you take a moment to appreciate something, no matter how small, it's like sprinkling a little bit of magic onto your life. The more you sprinkle, the shinier your life becomes. And who doesn't want a little extra shine?

Imagine walking through your day with a sparkle wand, touching everything you see with gratitude. Suddenly, that mundane cup of coffee becomes a comforting ritual, your commute becomes a time for reflection, and even the challenges you face start to reveal hidden blessings. Gratitude has the power to transform the ordinary into the extraordinary, turning your everyday moments into something truly special.

So, the next time you find yourself feeling stressed or overwhelmed, remember that you have a superpower at your disposal. Take a deep breath, think of something you're grateful for, and let those brain sparkles light up. Your brain—and your life—will thank you for it!

GRATITUDE CHECK-IN

GRATITUDE ISN'T ABOUT HAVING IT ALL; IT'S ABOUT LOVING WHAT YOU HAVE RIGHT NOW

Alright, before we dive deeper into the world of gratitude, let's do a quick check-in. Think of your gratitude levels like a gas tank in your car. Are you cruising along on a full tank, feeling abundant and appreciative of everything around you? Or maybe you're halfway there, feeling grateful for some things but struggling to see the bright side in others. Perhaps you're running on empty, finding it hard to muster up gratitude in the midst of life's challenges.

Whatever your current level, it's important to remember that there's no right or wrong place to be. This isn't a test; it's just a chance to see where you're starting from. Understanding your current gratitude level helps you know what areas need a little more attention and love. And just like with a car, if you find yourself running low, it's simply time to refuel.

Now, let's make this check-in even more tangible with a fun little exercise. Grab a notebook, or if you're more of a digital person, open up the notes app on your phone. Take a moment to think about three things you're grateful for right now. Don't overthink it—go with the first things that pop into your mind. They don't have to be profound or life-changing; sometimes, the simplest things bring the most joy.

Maybe you're grateful for that delicious cup of coffee you had this morning, the fact that you got a solid eight hours of sleep, or even that hilarious meme that made you laugh out loud. Whatever it is, jot it down. This exercise isn't about impressing anyone; it's about tuning into the everyday blessings that often go unnoticed.

See how easy that was? You've just taken your first step towards becoming a Gratitude Guru! It's a small but mighty action that can have a ripple effect on your entire day. The more you practice this, the more natural it will become, and soon, you'll find yourself spotting things to be grateful for everywhere you look.

WHY BEING A GRATITUDE GURU ROCKS

Now that you've dipped your toes in the gratitude pool, let's talk about why it's so awesome to be a Gratitude Guru. When you make gratitude a regular part of your life, something truly magical happens—your whole outlook on life begins to shift. Suddenly, you start to notice the good stuff more often, and the not-so-good stuff doesn't seem as overwhelming. It's like having a built-in happiness booster that you can activate anytime, anywhere.

Imagine this: you're having a rough day at work. Deadlines are looming, your inbox is overflowing, and nothing seems to be going right. But then you take a moment to pause and reflect on something you're grateful for. Maybe it's the fact that you have a job that challenges you, or the support of a colleague who always has your back. That small shift in perspective can make a world of difference, turning a stressful situation into an opportunity to appreciate the positive aspects of your life.

And here's the coolest part—gratitude is contagious. When you're radiating gratitude, the people around you start to pick up on it. Your positive vibes can lift up your friends, family, and even strangers. Have you ever noticed how a genuine smile or a kind word can brighten someone else's day? That's the power of gratitude in action. When you walk around like a human sunshine beam, spreading warmth and positivity, you create a ripple effect that can change not just your life but the lives of those around you.

Imagine being the person who, without even trying, makes other people feel good just by being around. That's the essence of a Gratitude Guru—someone who not only appreciates life's blessings but also spreads that appreciation far and wide. It's a superpower that doesn't just benefit you; it has the potential to transform entire communities.

LET'S GET OUR GRATITUDE GROOVE ON

So, how do you become a full-fledged Gratitude Guru? It's all about practice, practice, practice! Like any skill, the more you do it, the better you'll get. The great thing about gratitude is that it's easy to incorporate into your daily routine. Start small and build your way up with these fun and simple ideas:

Morning Gratitude Ritual:
Before you even get out of bed, think of one thing you're grateful for. It can be as simple as the comfy blanket you're wrapped in or the fact that you have a new day ahead of you. This sets a positive tone for the rest of your day.

Gratitude Walk:
Take a walk outside and look for things to be grateful for. Maybe it's the fresh air, the sound of birds singing, or the way the sun feels on your face. Every step can be a reminder of something good. Plus, walking itself is a great way to clear your mind and boost your mood.

Gratitude Jar:
Find a jar (or a box, or even a shoe—you do you!) and every day, write down something you're grateful for on a slip of paper and drop it in. Over time, you'll have a jar full of positivity that you can turn to whenever you need a pick-me-up.

Gratitude Buddy:
Team up with a friend or family member and share what you're grateful for with each other. It's a great way to stay motivated and spread the gratitude love. Plus, it deepens your connection with those you care about.

REMEMBER, THERE'S NO WRONG WAY TO PRACTICE GRATITUDE
The more you do it, the more natural it becomes

Remember, there's no wrong way to practice gratitude. The more you do it, the more natural it becomes, and before you know it, you'll be living life with the heart of a Gratitude Guru. It's not about being perfect; it's about making gratitude a regular part of your life, so it becomes second nature

YOUR GRATITUDE ADVENTURE BEGINS

EMBRACE YOUR INNER GURU INSIDE OF YOU! IT IS READY TO BE UNLEASHED!

So, are you ready to embrace your inner Gratitude Guru? This is just the beginning of an amazing adventure. As you move forward, keep your eyes, ears, and heart open to all the wonderful things around you. The more you practice, the more you'll discover just how powerful gratitude really is.

Your journey to a more joyful, abundant life starts now—let's make it sparkle! Every day is a new opportunity to fuel up your gratitude tank, and as you do, you'll find yourself cruising through life with more ease, joy, and fulfillment. So go ahead, start your engine, and let the gratitude adventure begin!

Let's make it sparkle!

YOUR VIBE REFLECTS WHAT YOU FOCUS ON—SO AIM FOR GRATITUDE, AND WATCH YOUR FREQUENCY RISE

Vibes Don't Lie: Understanding Energy Magic

CHAPTER 2

ENERGY 101 WITH A TWIST

When we talk about energy and vibration, it might sound a bit mystical or abstract, but let's break it down in a way that's easy to understand—think of it as the Wi-Fi signal for your soul. Just like your devices need a strong Wi-Fi connection to function at their best, your soul needs a high-vibe energy connection to thrive.

UNDERSTANDING ENERGY AND VIBRATION

At its core, everything in the universe is made up of energy. This includes your thoughts, emotions, and even your physical body. Energy is constantly moving and vibrating at different frequencies, and these vibrations can influence how you feel, how you think, and what you attract into your life. Think of your personal energy as the signal that connects you to the world around you.

When your energy is high and your vibrations are positive, it's like having a strong Wi-Fi signal—everything flows smoothly, you're in sync with the universe, and you easily attract the things you desire. But when your energy is low or your vibrations are off, it's like having a weak signal—things feel disconnected, and it's harder to manifest your goals or maintain a positive mindset.

TUNING INTO YOUR ENERGY

Just like you check your Wi-Fi signal to make sure it's strong, you can tune into your energy to see where you're at. Are you feeling energised, positive, and aligned? Or are you feeling drained, negative, or stuck? Your emotions, thoughts, and physical sensations are all indicators of your energy levels.

When you're vibrating at a high frequency—think of it as being in a good mood, feeling grateful, or being excited about life—your "soul signal" is strong. You're more connected to your true self, to others, and to the universe. This high-vibe state attracts more of the same positive energy back to you, creating a cycle of abundance, joy, and fulfilment.

On the other hand, when you're vibrating at a lower frequency—feeling stressed, anxious, or overwhelmed—your signal gets weaker. It's like trying to stream a video on a weak Wi-Fi connection: everything buffers, and it's harder to get anything done. This low-vibe state can make you feel disconnected from yourself and your goals, and it can attract more negative experiences into your life.

Check your Wi-Fi signal

BOOSTING YOUR SOUL'S WI-FI SIGNAL

Here's how!

The good news is that, just like you can move closer to a router to improve your Wi-Fi connection, you can take steps to boost your energy and raise your vibrations. Here's how:

Gratitude Practice:
Gratitude is like a signal booster for your soul. When you focus on what you're thankful for, you automatically raise your vibration and strengthen your connection to positive energy.

Mindfulness and Meditation:
These practices help you clear away the "noise" that can interfere with your signal. By calming your mind and focusing on the present moment, you create a clear, strong channel for high-vibe energy to flow.

Positive Thoughts and Emotions:
Your thoughts and emotions directly affect your vibration. By choosing to focus on positive, uplifting thoughts, you keep your energy high and your soul signal strong.

Healthy Living:
Taking care of your body with good nutrition, exercise, and plenty of rest ensures that your physical energy is in sync with your emotional and spiritual energy, keeping your overall vibration high.

Surrounding Yourself with High-Vibe People:
Just like being in a room with a strong Wi-Fi connection helps everyone get better service, surrounding yourself with positive, uplifting people can raise your own vibration

USING YOUR ENERGY WISELY

Understanding energy and vibration is like knowing how to manage your Wi-Fi network. You become more mindful of where you're putting your attention and energy, ensuring that you're not wasting your "signal" on things that drain you. Instead, you focus on what uplifts you, aligns with your goals, and supports your overall well-being.

By tuning into your energy and maintaining a high vibration, you're essentially keeping your soul's Wi-Fi signal strong and clear. This allows you to stay connected to your true self, attract positive experiences, and navigate life's challenges with ease.

So, the next time you're feeling a little "buffered" or disconnected, remember to check your soul's signal. Boost your energy, raise your vibration, and watch as your life begins to flow with more ease, joy, and synchronicity. With a strong Wi-Fi signal for your soul, there's no limit to what you can achieve!

HIGH VIBES ONLY
What Are Vibez, Anyway?

You've probably heard the phrase "good vibez only," but what does that really mean? And how do you know when you're experiencing good vibes versus bad vibez? Let's break it down in a way that's easy, fun, and totally relatable—so you can keep those high vibez flowing in your life.

WHAT ARE VIBEZ, ANYWAY?

Vibez, short for vibrations, are the energy frequencies that you give off and that you pick up from the world around you. Every person, place, and thing has a certain vibe, and those vibes can either uplift you or bring you down. Think of vibes as the emotional and energetic atmosphere that surrounds you. They can influence how you feel, how you think, and how you interact with others.

Imagine walking into a room where everyone is laughing and having a great time. You can feel the good vibez instantly—they're contagious, making you feel lighter, happier, and more connected. On the other hand, if you walk into a room where there's tension, people aren't speaking, or there's a lot of negativity, you can feel those bad vibez too. They might make you feel uncomfortable, anxious, or even drained.

GOOD VIBEZ: THE ENERGY OF POSITIVITY

Good vibez are all about positivity, joy, and alignment with your true self. When you're in a state of good vibez, you feel happy, confident, and at peace with the world. This high-vibe energy is infectious—it lifts you up and everyone around you, creating a ripple effect of positivity.

Here's what good vibez look and feel like:

Positive Emotions:
Happiness, gratitude, love, and excitement are all high-vibe emotions that contribute to good vibez. When you're feeling these emotions, your energy is elevated, and you're more likely to attract positive experiences.

Flow State:
When you're in the zone, fully engaged in an activity you love, you're in a flow state. This is a high-vibe place to be because you're completely aligned with what you're doing, and everything feels effortless.

Connection:
Good vibez often come from feeling connected—to yourself, to others, and to the world around you. This connection brings a sense of belonging and purpose, which naturally raises your vibration.

Lightness:
Ever notice how good vibez make you feel lighter, like you're floating on air? That's because high-vibe energy lifts you up, both physically and emotionally. You feel more energised, more creative, and more in tune with life.

BAD VIBEZ: THE ENERGY OF NEGATIVITY

Bad vibez, on the other hand, are the result of negativity, fear, and disconnection. When you're in a low-vibe state, you might feel stressed, anxious, or out of sync with yourself and your surroundings. Bad vibez can bring you down, making it harder to stay positive and motivated. Here's what bad vibez look and feel like:

Negative Emotions:
Fear, anger, jealousy, and sadness are all low-vibe emotions that contribute to bad vibes. These emotions can weigh you down, making you feel stuck or overwhelmed.

Resistance:
When you're resisting something—whether it's a situation, a person, or even your own feelings—you're creating bad vibes. Resistance creates tension and blocks the flow of positive energy.

Disconnection:
Bad vibez often come from feeling disconnected—from yourself, from others, and from the world around you. This disconnection can lead to loneliness, confusion, and a lack of purpose.

Heaviness:
Bad vibez have a way of making you feel heavy, like you're carrying a weight on your shoulders. This heaviness can drain your energy, leaving you feeling tired, unmotivated, and out of balance.

HOW TO STAY IN THE GOOD VIBEZ ZONE

Now that you know the difference between good vibes and bad vibez, let's talk about how to keep your energy high and your vibez positive. Here are some fun and easy ways to stay in the good vibez zone:

> **Gratitude IS Your Secret Superpower**

Surround Yourself with Positivity:
Spend time with people who lift you up and make you feel good. Fill your space with things that inspire you—like uplifting music, colourful artwork, or anything that brings you joy.

STAY IN GOOD VIBEZ
Keep your energy high

Practice Gratitude:
Gratitude is one of the quickest ways to shift your energy from low to high. Take a moment each day to reflect on what you're grateful for, and watch as your vibez naturally rise.

Move Your Body:
Physical movement is a great way to shake off bad vibez and get your energy flowing. Dance, go for a walk, or do some yoga—whatever feels good to you. Moving your body helps release tension and brings more lightness into your life.

Mind Your Thoughts:
Your thoughts have a huge impact on your vibez. When you notice negative or low-vibe thoughts creeping in, gently shift your focus to something positive. Affirmations, positive self-talk, and visualisation are great tools for keeping your thoughts high-vibe.

Create a High-Vibe Environment:
Your surroundings affect your energy, so make sure your environment supports good vibez. Keep your space clean, organised, and filled with things that make you feel happy and relaxed.

Protect Your Energy:
Sometimes, you can't avoid bad vibez—whether they come from other people or challenging situations. In these cases, it's important to protect your energy. Set boundaries, take breaks when needed, and don't be afraid to step away from situations that bring you down.

Good vibez aren't random—they're the result of choosing gratitude over doubt

MAKING GOOD VIBEZ A HABIT

The more you practice cultivating good vibez, the more natural it will become. Over time, staying in a high-vibe state will feel like second nature, and you'll find that it's easier to maintain your positivity and energy, even when faced with challenges.

Remember, vibez are contagious—when you're radiating good vibez, you not only uplift yourself but also everyone around you. So, keep choosing positivity, stay aligned with your true self, and make high vibez your new normal. Life is too short to be weighed down by bad vibez, so let's keep it light, keep it fun, and keep those good vibez flowing!

Vibez are contagious!

VIBE-O-METRE

Ever wondered where your vibez land on the frequency scale? Are you soaring high, radiating positivity, or could your energy use a little boost? The Vibe-O-Metre is a fun and simple self-assessment to help you gauge your current vibe level. Think of it as checking in on your energy, just like you might check the weather or your phone battery. Ready to find out where you stand? Let's dive into the activity!

You can also do this online, please visit:

https://api.leadconnectorhq.com/widget/quiz/lb5qCqccFLGO1zSXCCw2

HOW TO USE THE VIBE-O-METRE

The Vibe-O-Metre is designed to help you reflect on your current emotional and energetic state. It's a playful tool that encourages you to be honest with yourself—there are no right or wrong answers, just a chance to get in tune with how you're feeling right now.

Grab a pen and paper, or simply keep a mental note as you answer the following questions. Each question will have a point value associated with it, and at the end, you'll tally up your score to see where you land on the Vibe-O-Metre scale.

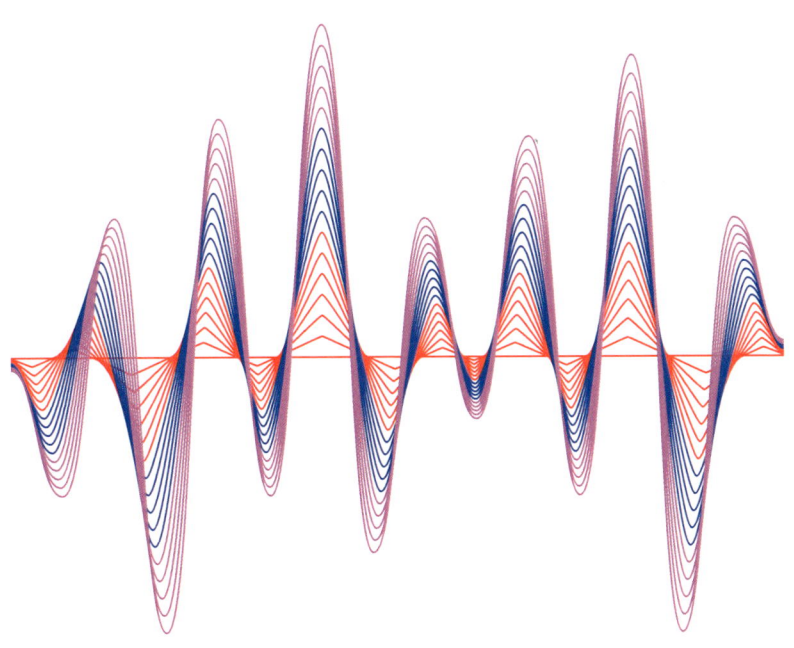

VIBE-O-METRE SELF-ASSESSMENT QUESTIONS

1. How do you feel when you wake up in the morning?
   - Energised and ready to take on the day! (10 points)
   - Pretty good, but I could use a little more sleep. (7 points)
   - Meh, just another day. (4 points)
   - Ugh, I wish I could stay in bed forever. (1 point)

2. How do you handle unexpected challenges?
   - I see them as opportunities to grow and learn. (10 points)
   - I try to stay positive, but it's not always easy. (7 points)
   - I get frustrated, but I eventually deal with them. (4 points)
   - I feel overwhelmed and struggle to cope. (1 point)

3. How often do you practice gratitude?
   - Every day, it's a big part of my routine. (10 points)
   - Most days, I try to remember to be thankful. (7 points)
   - Occasionally, but not as much as I'd like. (4 points)
   - Rarely, it's not something I think about often. (1 point)

4. What's your usual mood like during the day?
   - Happy, optimistic, and full of energy. (10 points)
   - Generally positive, with some ups and downs. (7 points)
   - Neutral, I just go with the flow. (4 points)
   - Often stressed, tired, or irritable. (1 point)

5. How do you feel in social situations?
   - Excited and energised by connecting with others. (10 points)
   - I enjoy it, but I also need some time alone to recharge. (7 points)
   - It depends on the day and who I'm with. (4 points)
   - Drained or anxious, I prefer to avoid them. (1 point)

6. How much do you enjoy the present moment?
   - I'm fully present and savouring every moment. (10 points)
   - I try to stay present, but my mind wanders sometimes. (7 points)
   - I'm often thinking about the past or worrying about the future. (4 points)
   - I rarely feel fully present; I'm usually distracted. (1 point)

7. How do you respond to negativity from others?
   - I stay positive and try not to let it affect me. (10 points)
   - I can shake it off most of the time. (7 points)
   - It bothers me, but I try to move past it. (4 points)
   - It really gets to me and brings my mood down. (1 point)

ADD UP YOUR POINTS

Now that you've answered the questions, it's time to tally up your points. Add the scores for each of your answers to get your total.

70–100 points: High Vibe Hero
- You're vibing high, and it shows! Your energy is radiant, positive, and contagious. You're in sync with yourself and the world around you, and you're likely attracting good things into your life. Keep doing what you're doing—your high vibez are a beacon of light for others!

40–69 points: Steady Vibe Seeker
- You're in a pretty good place, with a generally positive outlook and balanced energy. You might have a few ups and downs, but you're committed to maintaining your good vibez. With a little extra focus on self-care and positivity, you can raise your vibration even higher.

20–39 points: Vibe Tune-Up Needed
- Your vibez could use a little TLC. You might be feeling more neutral or low-energy than you'd like, and it's affecting how you experience life. Consider incorporating more high-vibe practices into your routine, like gratitude, mindfulness, and spending time with uplifting people.

7–19 points: Low Vibe Alert
- It seems like your vibez are currently on the low side, and that's okay—it happens to all of us sometimes. The important thing is to recognise it and take steps to raise your frequency. Focus on self-care, positivity, and reconnecting with the things that bring you joy.

BOOST YOUR VIBES BASED ON YOUR SCORE

No matter where you landed on the Vibe-O-Metre, there's always room for growth and improvement. If you're already riding high, keep those good vibez going strong by continuing your positive practices. If you scored lower than you'd like, don't worry—use it as an opportunity to make some changes and uplift your energy.
Here are a few tips to help you boost your vibez:

High Vibe Hero:
Keep spreading those good vibez! Share your positivity with others, continue practicing gratitude, and stay open to new opportunities that match your high energy.

Steady Vibe Seeker:
Focus on consistency in your vibe-boosting practices. Try setting aside more time for activities that uplift you, like spending time in nature, practicing mindfulness, or exploring creative outlets.

Vibe Tune-Up Needed:
Start small by integrating daily gratitude and mindfulness practices. Surround yourself with positivity, whether it's uplifting music, inspiring books, or supportive people. Remember, even small changes can make a big difference.

Low Vibe Alert:
Prioritise self-care and reconnect with activities that bring you joy and peace. It might help to take a break from stressors, practice deep breathing, or seek support from a friend or mentor. Focus on building your energy back up, one step at a time.

FINAL THOUGHTS: USE THE VIBE-O-METRE REGULARLY

The Vibe-O-Metre is a fun and insightful way to check in with yourself and see where your energy is at. Make it a regular part of your self-care routine to keep track of your vibes and stay aligned with your highest self. Remember, your energy is always within your control, and with a little awareness and intention, you can keep your vibez high, no matter what life throws your way.

Do your online quiz today, please visit:

https://api.leadconnectorhq.com/widget/quiz/lb5qCqccFLGO1zSXCCw2

THANKFULNESS UNLOCKS

ABUNDANCE

GRATITUDE GROWS

PROSPERITY

From Lack to Lavish: Flipping the Abundance Switch

CHAPTER 3

DITCH THE SCARCITY SYNDROME
Let's Talk...

Let's talk about something that sneaks into our minds more often than we realise—the scarcity syndrome. It's that little voice in your head that whispers, "There's not enough," "I'll never have what I need," or "If they have it, I can't." Whether it's about money, love, success, or even time, this mindset makes you feel like you're constantly coming up short, no matter what you do. But here's the truth: scarcity is a trick of the mind, and it's time to kick it to the kerb.

Scarcity syndrome is rooted in fear. It's the belief that life is a zero-sum game, where someone else's gain automatically means your loss. This mindset can leave you feeling anxious, competitive, and perpetually unsatisfied, always chasing more but never feeling like you have enough. And let's be real—that's no way to live!

Now, imagine living with the opposite mindset—an abundance mindset. Instead of seeing the world as full of limitations, you start to see it as overflowing with opportunities. Abundance is about believing that there's more than enough to go around, that the universe is generous, and that your needs will always be met. It's about trusting that good things are on their way to you, even if you can't see them yet.

So how do you ditch the scarcity syndrome and step into abundance? The answer lies in—you guessed it—gratitude. Gratitude is like a magic lens that transforms how you see the world. When you start focusing on what you have instead of what you lack, something incredible happens: you realize that you're already richer than you thought.

Here's how you can start shifting from scarcity to abundance:

Catch Yourself in the Act:
The next time you notice yourself thinking, "I don't have enough," or "I'm missing out," pause for a moment. Recognize that this is the scarcity syndrome talking. Awareness is the first step in changing any habit.

Flip the Script:
Once you've caught that scarcity thought, flip it around. Instead of focusing on what you don't have, think about what you do have. For example, if you're worried about money, shift your focus to the resources you already have—like your skills, your support network, or even the roof over your head.

Practice Daily Gratitude:
Make it a habit to start and end your day with gratitude. List three things you're grateful for every morning and every night. Over time, you'll train your brain to see abundance everywhere.

Celebrate Others:
One of the best ways to combat scarcity is to genuinely celebrate other people's successes. When you see someone else thriving, instead of feeling envious or threatened, feel happy for them. Remember, their success doesn't diminish your potential—it's proof that abundance is possible for everyone.

Give Freely:
Scarcity tells you to hold on tight to what you have, but abundance is all about flow. Practice giving—whether it's your time, money, or energy. When you give freely, you reinforce the belief that there's plenty to go around, and you'll start to see that what you give comes back to you multiplied.

Ditching the scarcity syndrome is like lifting a huge weight off your shoulders. You'll feel lighter, more optimistic, and more in control of your life. Remember, abundance isn't about having more stuff—it's about feeling fulfilled with what you have and trusting that more good things are always on the way. So, let go of the fear, embrace gratitude, and start living with a mindset of plenty. You've got this!

ACTIVATE ABUNDANCE MODE

Alright, it's time to take things up a notch and step into a whole new level of living—welcome to Abundance Mode! If you're ready to leave behind the limiting beliefs and scarcity mindset that have been holding you back, then activating Abundance Mode is your next move. This isn't just a mindset shift; it's a way of life where you align yourself with the flow of endless possibilities, opportunities, and blessings that are already available to you.

Think of Abundance Mode as flipping a switch in your mind. When it's on, you start to see the world differently. You notice opportunities where before you saw obstacles. You begin to attract positive experiences, people, and resources like a magnet. It's not magic; it's the power of your thoughts and beliefs aligning with the truth that the universe is full of abundance, and it's all there for you to tap into.

So, how do you flip that switch and activate Abundance Mode? Here are some practical steps to help you get started:

> **Gratitude is the key that unlocks life's abundance—when you give thanks, the universe gives more**

ACTIVATE ABUNDANCE MODE

Cultivate a "More Than Enough" Mindset
The first step to activating Abundance Mode is to embrace the belief that there is more than enough of everything you need—whether it's money, love, opportunities, or time. Start by affirming this belief daily. Say to yourself, "There is more than enough for me and everyone else," and really let that sink in. The more you reinforce this belief, the more you'll start to see evidence of it in your life.

Visualise Your Abundant Life
Visualisation is a powerful tool for activating Abundance Mode. Take a few minutes each day to close your eyes and imagine your life as if everything you desire has already come to pass. Picture yourself living in abundance—feeling secure, fulfilled, and joyful. How does it feel? What do you see? By consistently visualising your abundant life, you send a clear signal to the universe about what you want to attract.

Speak the Language of Abundance
Your words are incredibly powerful. They shape your reality and influence how you see the world. To activate Abundance Mode, start speaking the language of abundance. Replace phrases like "I can't afford that" with "I choose to spend my money differently right now" or "I'm investing in other areas." Shift from saying "I don't have enough time" to "I have plenty of time to accomplish what's important to me." The words you use create the energy you live in, so choose words that reflect abundance.

Surround Yourself with Abundance
Look around you—what are the things, people, and environments you're surrounding yourself with? Are they reinforcing scarcity or abundance? To activate Abundance Mode, start filling your life with things that represent abundance to you. This could mean decluttering your space to make room for new opportunities, spending time with positive and uplifting people, or immersing yourself in environments that inspire and energise you.

Practice Generosity

One of the most powerful ways to activate Abundance Mode is through giving. When you give freely—whether it's your time, money, or talents—you're sending a clear message to the universe that you believe in abundance. Generosity creates a flow of energy that brings more of what you give back to you. It reinforces the idea that there's always more where that came from, and it opens the door for abundance to flow into your life.

Be Grateful for What You Have

Gratitude is the foundation of abundance. The more you appreciate what you already have, the more you'll attract into your life. Take time each day to reflect on what you're grateful for, no matter how big or small. This simple practice shifts your focus from lack to abundance and helps you realise just how rich you already are. When you're grateful, you're in the perfect state to receive even more.

Trust the Process

Finally, activating Abundance Mode requires trust. Trust that the universe has your back, that good things are on their way, and that you are exactly where you need to be. Trust that when you focus on abundance, it will naturally flow into your life. Let go of the need to control every outcome and have faith that abundance is your birthright.

When you activate Abundance Mode, you're not just wishing for more—you're creating a mindset and a lifestyle that naturally attracts more of what you desire. It's about stepping into a space where you're open to receiving all the good things the universe has to offer. So go ahead, flip that switch, and watch as abundance starts to show up in every area of your life. The universe is ready to deliver—are you ready to receive?

Gratitude attracts miracles

GRATITUDE GAME PLAN

Ready to take your gratitude practice to the next level? It's time to put together a Gratitude Game Plan—a simple, effective strategy that will help you cultivate gratitude consistently, no matter what life throws your way. Just like any other important goal, having a plan in place makes it easier to stay on track and make gratitude a natural part of your daily routine.

Think of this game plan as your personal blueprint for living a more joyful, abundant life. It's designed to fit seamlessly into your day, so you can start experiencing the transformative power of gratitude right away. Here's how to get started:

Start Your Day with Gratitude
The way you start your day sets the tone for everything that follows. That's why the first step in your Gratitude Game Plan is to begin each morning with a gratitude ritual. Before you even get out of bed, take a moment to think of one thing you're grateful for. It doesn't have to be anything grand—something as simple as the comfort of your bed, the opportunity to start a new day, or the sound of birds chirping outside your window works perfectly.
This simple practice immediately puts you in a positive mindset and helps you approach the day with an attitude of appreciation. As you get more comfortable with this ritual, you can expand it by thinking of three things you're grateful for each morning. The key is consistency—starting your day with gratitude sets you up for success.

Incorporate Gratitude Breaks Throughout the Day
Just like taking coffee breaks or stretching your legs, incorporating gratitude breaks into your day can make a big difference in how you feel. Set aside a few minutes during your day to pause, take a deep breath, and reflect on something you're grateful for in that moment.
These gratitude breaks don't need to be long or complicated. Maybe it's a quick acknowledgment of a kind word from a colleague, the taste of your favorite snack, or the satisfaction of completing a task. By regularly checking in with yourself and practicing gratitude, you'll find that it becomes easier to maintain a positive outlook, even on busy or challenging days.

End Your Day with Gratitude
Just as you start your day with gratitude, it's important to end it on a similar note. Before you go to sleep, take a few moments to reflect on your day and jot down three things you're grateful for. This practice not only helps you unwind but also reinforces the positive experiences you had throughout the day, no matter how small they may seem.

Create a Gratitude Jar

Here's a fun and visual way to keep track of your gratitude—create a Gratitude Jar. Find a jar, box, or any container that you like, and place it somewhere you'll see every day. Whenever you feel grateful for something, write it down on a small piece of paper and drop it into the jar.

Over time, your Gratitude Jar will fill up with positive memories, blessings, and little moments of joy. On days when you're feeling down or need a reminder of the good in your life, you can reach into the jar and read through some of the notes. It's a tangible way to see just how much you have to be thankful for, and it's a great motivator to keep practicing gratitude.

Share Your Gratitude with Others

Gratitude isn't just something you keep to yourself—it's meant to be shared. Make it a point to express your gratitude to the people in your life, whether it's through a kind word, a thank-you note, or simply telling someone how much you appreciate them. Not only does this strengthen your relationships, but it also spreads positivity and encourages others to practice gratitude as well.

You can even take this a step further by creating a Gratitude Buddy system. Team up with a friend or family member and regularly share what you're grateful for with each other. This can be through daily texts, weekly calls, or even a shared journal. Having someone to share your gratitude with makes the practice more enjoyable and helps you stay committed to it.

Practice Gratitude in Challenging Times

It's easy to feel grateful when things are going well, but the true power of gratitude lies in its ability to uplift you during tough times. When you're faced with challenges, take a moment to find something—anything—to be grateful for. It might be the lesson you're learning, the strength you're gaining, or the support you're receiving from others.

Practicing gratitude in difficult moments doesn't mean ignoring or minimizing your struggles. Instead, it's about finding a glimmer of hope or a silver lining, no matter how small. This shift in perspective can help you navigate challenges with more resilience and grace.

Reflect and Celebrate Your Gratitude Wins

Finally, take time to reflect on your gratitude journey and celebrate your wins. Whether it's noticing a positive change in your mood, deepening your relationships, or simply maintaining your gratitude practice for a month, every step forward is worth acknowledging.

Consider keeping a gratitude journal where you can track your progress and reflect on how your practice has impacted your life. Celebrate the little milestones along the way, and remember that gratitude is a lifelong journey. The more you practice, the more natural it becomes, and the more abundance you'll attract into your life.

PUTTING IT ALL TOGETHER

Your Gratitude Game Plan is your roadmap to a more joyful, fulfilling life. By incorporating these practices into your daily routine, you'll start to notice a shift in how you experience the world. Gratitude will become second nature, and you'll find yourself living with a heart full of appreciation and a mind open to endless possibilities.

So, are you ready to get started? Take that first step today, and watch as your life begins to sparkle with the magic of gratitude. You've got the plan—now it's time to put it into action and embrace the abundance that's waiting for you!

When you appreciate the journey, success is inevitable

Imagine this: you're having a rough day at work. Deadlines are looming, your inbox is overflowing, and nothing seems to be going right. But then you take a moment to pause and reflect on something you're grateful for. Maybe it's the fact that you have a job that challenges you, or the support of a colleague who always has your back. That small shift in perspective can make a world of difference, turning a stressful situation into an opportunity to appreciate the positive aspects of your life.

And here's the coolest part—gratitude is contagious. When you're radiating gratitude, the people around you start to pick up on it. Your positive vibes can lift up your friends, family, and even strangers. Have you ever noticed how a genuine smile or a kind word can brighten someone else's day? That's the power of gratitude in action. When you walk around like a human sunshine beam, spreading warmth and positivity, you create a ripple effect that can change not just your life but the lives of those around you.

Imagine being the person who, without even trying, makes other people feel good just by being around. That's the essence of a Gratitude Guru—someone who not only appreciates life's blessings but also spreads that appreciation far and wide. It's a superpower that doesn't just benefit you; it has the potential to transform entire communities.

LET'S GET OUR GRATITUDE GROOVE ON

So, how do you become a full-fledged Gratitude Guru? It's all about practice, practice, practice! Like any skill, the more you do it, the better you'll get. The great thing about gratitude is that it's easy to incorporate into your daily routine. Start small and build your way up with these fun and simple ideas:

Morning Gratitude Ritual:
Before you even get out of bed, think of one thing you're grateful for. It can be as simple as the comfy blanket you're wrapped in or the fact that you have a new day ahead of you. This sets a positive tone for the rest of your day.

Gratitude Walk:
Take a walk outside and look for things to be grateful for. Maybe it's the fresh air, the sound of birds singing, or the way the sun feels on your face. Every step can be a reminder of something good. Plus, walking itself is a great way to clear your mind and boost your mood.

Gratitude Jar:
Find a jar (or a box, or even a shoe—you do you!) and every day, write down something you're grateful for on a slip of paper and drop it in. Over time, you'll have a jar full of positivity that you can turn to whenever you need a pick-me-up.

Gratitude Buddy:
Team up with a friend or family member and share what you're grateful for with each other. It's a great way to stay motivated and spread the gratitude love. Plus, it deepens your connection with those you care about.

GRATITUDE ISN'T JUST A FEELING—IT'S A FREQUENCY. WHEN YOU TUNE IN, ABUNDANCE ANSWERS BACK

Gratitude, Unplugged: Creating Your Personal Practice

CHAPTER 4

BUILD YOUR GRATITUDE GROOVE
Let's Make Moves

It's time to get into the groove—the Gratitude Groove, that is! Think of this as finding your rhythm in life where gratitude becomes a natural, effortless part of your everyday routine. Just like any good groove, it's all about consistency and flow. When you build your Gratitude Groove, you're setting yourself up for a life that's rich in positivity, joy, and abundance. So, let's dive into how you can create a groove that sticks!

Start Small and Simple
The best grooves start with a simple beat, right? The same goes for your Gratitude Groove. Don't feel like you need to overhaul your entire life to start practicing gratitude. Begin with something small and manageable. For example, you might decide to jot down one thing you're grateful for each morning. It could be anything—waking up feeling rested, the first sip of your coffee, or even just the fact that you have a new day ahead of you.

The key here is to start with something you can easily stick to. The simpler it is, the more likely you are to keep it going, and soon enough, it'll become as natural as brushing your teeth.

Find Your Gratitude Rhythm
Once you've got the basics down, it's time to find your rhythm. Your Gratitude Groove should be something that fits seamlessly into your daily life, not something that feels forced or like a chore. Take a look at your daily routine and find a natural spot where gratitude can flow in.

Maybe it's during your morning commute, where you can mentally list things you're grateful for. Or perhaps it's right before bed, when you take a few moments to reflect on your day and the good things that happened. The more you integrate gratitude into your existing routine, the easier it becomes to maintain your groove.

Make It Fun and Enjoyable
Your Gratitude Groove should feel good—like a song you can't help but dance to. Find ways to make your gratitude practice something you look forward to. You could start a gratitude journal with colourful pens, stickers, or doodles to make it more fun. Or, if you're more into tech, try a gratitude app that sends you daily reminders and lets you track your progress.

If you enjoy nature, consider combining your gratitude practice with a daily walk outside. As you walk, take in the sights and sounds around you and think about what you're grateful for. When you associate gratitude with something you love, it becomes a positive experience that you're eager to repeat.

Involve Your Senses
Want to deepen your Gratitude Groove? Engage your senses in your practice. Gratitude isn't just a mental exercise—it's something you can feel in your body, see in your surroundings, taste in your food, hear in your favourite music, and smell in a fresh bouquet of flowers.

For example, when you express gratitude for your morning coffee, don't just think it—take a moment to really savour the aroma, the warmth of the mug in your hands, and the rich flavour on your tongue. By involving your senses, you're amplifying the experience and making your gratitude practice more immersive and impactful.

Keep It Fresh and Evolving
Like any good groove, your Gratitude Groove should evolve over time. What works for you now might need a tweak later on, and that's okay. Keep things fresh by trying new gratitude practices and exploring different ways to express your appreciation.

Share the Groove
Gratitude is even more powerful when it's shared. Once you've built your Gratitude Groove, invite others to join in. Share your gratitude practice with friends or family members, and encourage them to find their own groove. You could even start a gratitude group where you meet regularly to discuss what you're grateful for and support each other in your practices.

Sharing your groove not only strengthens your own practice but also spreads positivity to those around you. It's like turning up the volume on your favourite song—everyone around you can't help but start tapping their toes, too!

READY TO GROOVE

Building your Gratitude Groove is about finding a rhythm that works for you—a practice that feels natural, enjoyable, and easy to maintain. It's not about perfection; it's about consistency and flow. The more you practice, the more ingrained it becomes, until gratitude is just a part of who you are.

So, are you ready to find your Gratitude Groove? Start small, make it fun, and watch as your life begins to dance to the beat of gratitude. With your groove in place, you'll find yourself moving through life with more joy, peace, and abundance. Let's get grooving!

THE ART OF GRATITUDE JOURNALING

boost Your Mood...

Welcome to the world of gratitude journaling—a simple yet transformative practice that can shift your perspective, boost your mood, and help you live a more joyful, abundant life. If you've ever felt overwhelmed by life's challenges or found yourself focusing on what's missing rather than what's present, then gratitude journaling might just be the tool you need to bring more positivity into your day-to-day experience.

Gratitude journaling is more than just writing down a few nice thoughts; it's about intentionally creating a space where you can reflect on the good in your life, no matter how big or small. It's an art form, one that you can personalise and make your own, allowing it to fit seamlessly into your lifestyle and meet your unique needs. In this chapter, we'll dive deep into the art of gratitude journaling—why it works, how to do it, and how to keep it fresh and inspiring.

WHY GRATITUDE JOURNALING WORKS

Before we get into the how, let's talk about the why. Why should you take the time to write down things you're grateful for? Well, it turns out that putting pen to paper (or fingers to keyboard) has some pretty powerful effects on your brain and overall well-being.

When you write down what you're grateful for, you're not just thinking about it—you're actively engaging with those thoughts. This process helps reinforce positive neural pathways in your brain, making it easier to focus on the good in your life. Over time, this practice can help rewire your brain to be more positive, more resilient, and more attuned to the abundance that surrounds you.

Gratitude journaling also serves as a tangible reminder of the good things in your life. On tough days, when you're feeling down or overwhelmed, you can look back through your journal and remember all the things you've been grateful for in the past. It's like having a personal treasure chest of positivity that you can dip into whenever you need a boost.

GETTING STARTED WITH GRATITUDE JOURNALING

If you're new to gratitude journaling, don't worry—it's super easy to get started. All you need is a notebook, a pen, and a few minutes of your time. Here's a simple step-by-step guide to help you begin:

Choose Your Journal: The first step is to find a journal that you love. It could be a fancy leather-bound notebook, a simple spiral-bound pad, or even a digital app on your phone. The key is to choose something that feels right for you—something you'll look forward to opening up every day.

Set Aside Time: Decide when you're going to do your gratitude journaling. Many people find it helpful to journal first thing in the morning to start the day on a positive note, or right before bed to reflect on the day's events. Choose a time that fits naturally into your routine.

Start Small: Begin by writing down three things you're grateful for each day. These don't have to be grand or life-changing—sometimes, the simplest things bring the most joy. It could be the taste of your morning coffee, a kind word from a friend, or the comfort of your favorite sweater. The key is to be consistent.

Be Specific: The more specific you are in your gratitude journal, the more impactful the practice will be. Instead of just writing, "I'm grateful for my family," try something like, "I'm grateful for the way my partner made me laugh today," or "I'm grateful for my child's excitement when they saw their favorite toy." Specificity helps you relive those positive moments and deepens your sense of appreciation.

Write from the Heart: Let your gratitude journal be a space where you can express yourself freely. Don't worry about grammar, spelling, or how your writing sounds—this journal is for you, and the most important thing is that it feels authentic. Write as if you're having a conversation with yourself or with a trusted friend.

KEEPING YOUR GRATITUDE JOURNAL FRESH

One of the keys to sticking with gratitude journaling is to keep it interesting and enjoyable. Here are some ideas to help you keep your gratitude practice fresh:

Mix Up Your Prompts:
While writing down three things you're grateful for each day is a great start, don't be afraid to mix things up with different prompts. For example:
- "What's one thing that made you smile today?"
- "What's something you're looking forward to?"
- "Who's someone you're grateful for and why?"
- "What's a challenge you're grateful for because it helped you grow?"

Changing up your prompts can help you see your life from different angles and keep your journaling sessions engaging.

Include Visuals: Sometimes, a picture really is worth a thousand words. If you're a visual person, consider adding photos, doodles, or even clippings from magazines that represent what you're grateful for. This can make your journal even more personal and creative.

Create Themes: Dedicate certain days or weeks to specific themes of gratitude. For example, you might focus on relationships one week, nature the next, and personal achievements the week after. This helps you dive deeper into specific areas of your life and explore gratitude in different contexts.

Share Your Gratitude: While your journal is a personal space, sharing some of your entries with a trusted friend or family member can enhance your experience. It's a great way to connect with others and spread positivity.

Review and Reflect: Every so often, take time to go back and read through your previous entries. Reflect on how far you've come, the patterns you notice, and the growth you've experienced. This reflection not only reinforces your gratitude practice but also gives you a sense of accomplishment and perspective.

GRATITUDE JOURNALING FOR TOUGH TIMES

Gratitude journaling isn't just for the good days—it's a powerful tool to help you navigate challenging times as well. When life gets tough, your gratitude journal can be a lifeline, helping you find the silver linings and stay grounded in what's positive.

On difficult days, try to focus on the small things that are going right, even if they seem insignificant. It might be the fact that you got out of bed, that you received a text from a friend checking in, or that you had a moment of peace during a hectic day. Remember, gratitude isn't about ignoring the tough stuff—it's about finding light in the darkness.

If you're struggling to find something to be grateful for, that's okay too. Use your journal to explore your feelings, and acknowledge where you are. Often, just the act of writing can help you process emotions and shift your perspective.

EMBRACE THE JOURNEY

The art of gratitude journaling is a journey, not a destination. It's about building a habit that supports your well-being and enriches your life, one entry at a time. The more you practice, the more natural it will become, and the more you'll start to notice the positive effects in your daily life.
So, grab your journal, find a quiet spot, and start writing. Let this be your sacred space—a place where you can cultivate gratitude, reflect on your blessings, and create a more joyful, abundant life. Your gratitude journal is your canvas—paint it with the colours of appreciation, love, and positivity, and watch as it transforms your world.

GRATITUDE ON THE GO

Let's face it—life can be a whirlwind. Between juggling work, family, and all the little things that fill up your day, it's easy to feel like there's no time left for yourself, let alone for something like practicing gratitude. But here's a little secret: you don't need to carve out hours of your day to feel grateful. You can practice gratitude on the go, weaving it into your daily routine like a thread of sunshine that brightens even the busiest of days.

Gratitude on the Go is all about finding those little pockets of time in your day where you can pause for a moment and appreciate what's around you. It's not about making a big effort or adding something else to your to-do list. Instead, it's about simple, easy habits that fit seamlessly into what you're already doing.

Let's start with mornings. As soon as you wake up, before you even roll out of bed, take a quick moment to think of something you're grateful for. It doesn't have to be anything profound—maybe it's just the cozy feeling of your blankets, the sound of birds chirping outside, or the fact that you have a brand-new day ahead of you. This tiny habit takes just a few seconds but can set a positive tone for the rest of your day. If you want to go a step further, you could turn it into a mini routine by thinking of three things you're grateful for each morning. It's like giving your day a head start on the right foot.

As you move through your day, there are plenty of opportunities to sneak in a little gratitude. While you're sipping your morning coffee or tea, take a moment to really savor it. Notice the warmth of the cup in your hands, the rich aroma, and the comforting taste. As you do, silently say a quick "thank you" for this small pleasure. This turns an ordinary moment into something special, simply by focusing on what you appreciate about it.

Commuting is another great time to practice gratitude on the go. Whether you're driving, taking the bus, or walking, you can use this time to reflect on the things you're thankful for. Maybe it's the fact that you have reliable transportation, or that you're headed to a job that supports you. Or perhaps it's something as simple as the music or podcast you're listening to, or the sights you pass along the way. By turning your commute into a time for gratitude, you can transform what might otherwise be a stressful part of your day into a peaceful and positive experience.

Throughout your workday, there are countless moments when you can pause for a quick gratitude check-in. When you finish a task, take a second to appreciate the sense of accomplishment. When a colleague helps you out, mentally thank them for their support. Even during meetings or busy moments, you can find something to be grateful for—whether it's the collaboration, the learning experience, or just the fact that you're able to contribute.

Lunch breaks offer another perfect opportunity for a gratitude break. As you eat, take a moment to appreciate your food—the flavours, the nourishment, and the fact that you have something to eat. If you're enjoying your lunch with others, be grateful for their company and the chance to connect. Even if you're eating alone, you can appreciate the quiet time to recharge.

As the day winds down, use your evening routine as a time to reflect on the good things that happened. While brushing your teeth or getting ready for bed, think back on your day and find a few moments that made you smile or feel good. It could be a kind word from a friend, the way the sunset looked, or simply that you made it through a tough day. This quick reflection can help you end your day on a positive note and make it easier to relax and sleep well.

The beauty of Gratitude on the Go is that it doesn't require any extra time or effort. It's about making the most of the moments you already have, and finding little ways to remind yourself of the good things in your life. The more you practice, the more natural it will become, and soon you'll find yourself feeling grateful without even thinking about it.

So, the next time you're rushing through your day, remember that gratitude is right there with you, ready to be noticed and appreciated. It's as easy as taking a breath, looking around, and saying "thank you" for the small joys and blessings that are always within reach.

THIS IS YOUR JOURNEY—WALK IT WITH GRATITUDE, AND EVERY STEP WILL BE A BLESSING

MAKING GOOD VIBEZ A HABIT

The more you practice cultivating good vibes, the more natural it will become. Over time, staying in a high-vibe state will feel like second nature, and you'll find that it's easier to maintain your positivity and energy, even when faced with challenges.

Remember, vibez are contagious—when you're radiating good vibez, you not only uplift yourself but also everyone around you. So, keep choosing positivity, stay aligned with your true self, and make high vibez your new normal. Life is too short to be weighed down by bad vibes, so let's keep it light, keep it fun, and keep those good vibez flowing!

Vibez are contagious!

GRATITUDE
Vibez

EVERY THANK YOU IS LIKE A MAGNET, PULLING IN MORE JOY, SUCCESS, AND MAGIC

CHAPTER 5

The Manifestation Frequency: Tuning into the Good Life

MANIFESTING 101

Welcome to Manifesting 101—the basics of turning your dreams into reality. You've probably heard the word "manifesting" tossed around a lot, especially in the world of self-improvement, but what does it actually mean? And more importantly, how do you do it? Well, you're about to find out that manifesting is simpler than you might think, and it all starts with a little shift in how you see the world.

Manifesting is essentially about bringing something you desire into your life through focus, belief, and action. It's the process of turning your thoughts and intentions into real-life experiences. Think of it as planting seeds in a garden—your thoughts and beliefs are the seeds, and with the right care and attention, they grow into the reality you want to experience.

But before we get into the how, let's start with the what. What do you want to manifest? It could be anything—a new job, better relationships, improved health, more money, or even just a greater sense of happiness and peace. The key to manifesting is to get clear on what you want. Imagine placing an order at a restaurant. You wouldn't just say, "Bring me food." You'd specify what you're craving. Manifesting works the same way—the more specific you are about what you want, the better.

Now, let's talk about the mindset behind manifesting. At its core, manifesting is about believing that what you want is possible and that you deserve to have it. This might sound obvious, but it's amazing how often we get in our own way with doubt, fear, and limiting beliefs. If you think, "I'd love a new job, but I'm not sure I'm good enough," you're already putting up a roadblock. Manifesting requires you to trust that the universe has your back and that what you want is already on its way to you.

So, how do you start manifesting? The first step is to set a clear intention. This is like drawing a map for where you want to go. Take some time to really think about what you want, and then write it down. Be as specific as you can—don't just say, "I want to be happy." Instead, describe what happiness looks like for you. Is it spending more time with family? Travelling the world? Doing work that you love? The clearer your intention, the more powerfully you can manifest it.

Once you've set your intention, it's time to focus on it. This doesn't mean obsessing over it or worrying about how it will happen. Instead, it's about keeping your intention in your mind and heart with a sense of calm confidence. You can do this through visualisation—imagine yourself already living the life you want. Picture it in as much detail as possible, and really feel the emotions that come with it. If you're manifesting a new job, imagine yourself walking into your new office, feeling excited and fulfilled. If it's better health, picture yourself full of energy, enjoying activities you love.

But here's the thing—manifesting isn't just about thinking. It's also about doing. Action is a crucial part of the manifesting process. You can't just sit back and wait for your dreams to show up at your door; you need to take steps towards them. If you're manifesting a new job, start updating your resume, networking, or applying for positions. If you're manifesting better health, start incorporating small, healthy habits into your daily routine. The actions don't have to be big, but they do need to be consistent. Each step you take is like watering the seeds you've planted, helping them grow.

Another important part of manifesting is letting go of the "how." This can be tricky because we often want to control every detail, but part of manifesting is trusting that the universe will handle the specifics. Your job is to stay focused on what you want and take inspired action, but leave the exact how and when up to the universe. This doesn't mean you don't have a say—it just means you're open to the many different ways your desires can come to you, some of which you might not have even considered.

One of the best ways to keep your manifesting game strong is through gratitude. Gratitude is like a magnet for more good things. When you're grateful for what you already have, you're sending a powerful message to the universe that you're ready for more. So, as you work on manifesting your desires, take time each day to appreciate what you already have. This could be anything from your morning coffee to the roof over your head to the people in your life. The more you focus on gratitude, the more you'll find to be grateful for, and the easier it will be to manifest your dreams.

Finally, remember that manifesting is a journey, not a race. It's about aligning your thoughts, beliefs, and actions with what you want and then trusting that it will come to you in the right time and way. Be patient with yourself, stay open to possibilities, and most importantly, enjoy the process. Every step you take is bringing you closer to the life you desire, and that's something to be excited about.

So, whether you're new to manifesting or you've been practicing it for a while, know that you have the power to create the life you want. It all starts with a clear intention, a positive mindset, and a willingness to take action. Get ready to plant those seeds, water them with belief and action, and watch as your dreams start to blossom. Happy manifesting!

Dream big, but don't forget— gratitude is the spark that turns dreams into reality!

VISUALISE, GRATIFY, MANIFEST

Welcome to the next step in your manifesting journey—Visualise, Gratify, Manifest. This three-step process is like a recipe for bringing your dreams to life, and it's as simple as it is powerful. If you've ever wondered how to turn your thoughts and desires into reality, this chapter will show you exactly how to do it.
Let's break it down:

Step 1: Visualise
The first step is visualisation. Visualisation is all about creating a vivid mental image of the life you want to live or the goals you want to achieve. It's like daydreaming, but with purpose. When you visualise, you're essentially giving your brain a blueprint of what you want to create. The more detailed and specific your visualisation, the more powerful it becomes.

Start by finding a quiet place where you won't be disturbed. Close your eyes and take a few deep breaths to relax. Now, think about what you want to manifest. It could be anything—a new job, a healthy body, a loving relationship, or a sense of inner peace. Picture it in your mind as if it's already happening. Imagine the sights, sounds, and even the smells associated with this reality. If you're visualising a new job, see yourself in your new workspace, interacting with colleagues, and feeling fulfilled. If it's better health, imagine yourself feeling energetic, enjoying your favourite activities, and radiating vitality.

The key is to make your visualisation as detailed as possible. The more you can immerse yourself in the experience, the more real it will feel, and the more likely it is to manifest. Don't just see it—feel it. Tap into the emotions you would have if this were already your reality. Feel the excitement, joy, peace, or satisfaction. This emotional connection is what makes visualisation so powerful because it signals to your brain that this is something important to you.

Step 2: Gratify
Now that you've visualised your desired outcome, it's time to add a layer of gratitude. Gratitude is like the secret sauce that makes your visualisation even more effective. When you express gratitude for something as if it's already happened, you're aligning yourself with the energy of receiving. It's like telling the universe, "Yes, I'm ready for this!"

After your visualisation, take a moment to feel genuinely grateful for the experience you just imagined. Say to yourself, "Thank you for this new job," or "Thank you for my vibrant health," or whatever it is you're manifesting. The trick here is to feel the gratitude as if your desire has already come true. This might feel a bit strange at first—thanking the universe for something that hasn't happened yet—but this is where the magic happens

More than enough

Gratitude shifts your focus from lack to abundance. Instead of dwelling on what you don't have, you're celebrating what you're creating. This positive energy not only boosts your mood but also sends a clear message to the universe that you're open to receiving what you've visualised. The more grateful you are, the more you attract things to be grateful for. It's like turning on a magnet that draws good things into your life.

Step 3: Manifest
The final step is to manifest—allowing what you've visualised and gratified to come into your life. This is where the rubber meets the road. Manifesting isn't just about sitting back and waiting for things to happen; it's about taking inspired action that aligns with your vision. When you've clearly visualised what you want and expressed gratitude for it, you'll start to notice opportunities and ideas that can help you bring it to life.

Manifesting is about being open and ready to act on these opportunities. It's about trusting that the universe will provide the "how" while you focus on the "what." Keep your eyes open for signs, synchronicities, and nudges from your intuition. Maybe you'll hear about a job opening through a friend, stumble upon a new workout that energises you, or meet someone who shares your goals. When these opportunities arise, take action! Even small steps can lead to big changes.

Remember, manifesting is a journey, not a destination. It's about staying in tune with your vision, maintaining an attitude of gratitude, and taking consistent action towards your goals. Some manifestations might happen quickly, while others take time to unfold. The key is to stay patient, keep believing, and continue taking steps in the right direction.

Gratitude attracts miracles

MANIFESTATION MAGIC TRICKS
Wave the wand...

One of the most important things to remember is that manifesting isn't just about getting what you want—it's about becoming the person who naturally attracts those things into your life. As you practice Visualise, Gratify, and Manifest, you'll start to notice shifts not only in what you receive but also in how you see yourself and the world around you. You'll become more confident, more optimistic, and more in tune with the flow of life.

So, are you ready to put this three-step process into action? Start today by setting aside a few minutes to visualise your dreams, express gratitude for them as if they've already come true, and be open to the opportunities that come your way. The more you practice, the easier it will become, and soon you'll see that manifesting isn't just a possibility—it's a way of life.

Get ready to visualise, gratify, and manifest the life of your dreams!

MANIFESTATION MAGIC TRICKS

Welcome to the fun and mystical world of Manifestation Magic Tricks! Think of these tricks as little hacks that can supercharge your manifesting powers and help you bring your dreams to life even faster. Whether you're new to manifesting or you've been practicing it for a while, these tips and techniques will add some extra sparkle to your journey. Ready to add some magic to your manifesting?
Let's dive in!

THE POWER OF AFFIRMATIONS

One of the easiest and most powerful manifestation magic tricks is using affirmations. Affirmations are positive statements that you repeat to yourself to help shift your mindset and align your thoughts with what you want to create. The key to effective affirmations is to phrase them as if what you want is already happening.

For example, instead of saying, "I want to be successful," you would say, "I am successful." Instead of "I hope to find love," you'd say, "I am surrounded by love." This might feel a bit strange at first, but the more you repeat these affirmations, the more your mind starts to believe them, and that belief creates the foundation for manifesting your desires.

Try incorporating affirmations into your daily routine. You can say them in the morning to start your day on a positive note or at night to set the tone for your dreams. You can even write them on sticky notes and place them around your home or workspace as little reminders throughout the day. The more you affirm what you want, the more you attract it into your life.

VISUALISATION WITH A TWIST

We've already talked about the power of visualisation, but here's a little twist that can make it even more effective: add motion and emotion to your visualisations. Instead of just seeing a still picture of your desired outcome, imagine it as if it's happening in real-time, like a movie playing in your mind.

We've already talked about the power of visualisation, but here's a little twist that can make it even more effective: add motion and emotion to your visualisations. Instead of just seeing a still picture of your desired outcome, imagine it as if it's happening in real-time, like a movie playing in your mind.

For example, if you're visualising a new home, don't just picture the house—see yourself walking through it, opening the front door, and feeling the excitement of moving in. Imagine the smell of fresh paint, the sound of your footsteps on the floor, and the joy of making it your own. The more senses you involve, the more real it becomes, and the stronger the manifesting power.

To take it up a notch, add emotions to your visualisation. Feel the happiness, pride, peace, or whatever emotions you'd experience if your visualisation were already your reality. Emotion is the secret ingredient that gives your visualisation extra power and makes it resonate more deeply with your subconscious mind.

THE "ACT AS IF" TRICK

Here's a fun one: start acting as if you already have what you want. This doesn't mean going out and spending money you don't have or pretending to be something you're not. Instead, it's about embodying the energy of the person who already has what you desire.

If you're manifesting a new job, start dressing the part and carrying yourself with the confidence of someone who already has that job. If you're manifesting more abundance, practice generosity and act with the mindset of someone who feels financially secure. This trick is all about aligning your behaviour with your desired outcome, which helps attract it into your life faster.

The "Act As If" trick works because it signals to your brain that you're already living the life you want. Your mind starts to look for evidence that supports this new reality, and you begin to attract the people, opportunities, and resources that match your new mindset.

Gratitude is the wand, and your belief is the spell—magic is inevitable when they work together

GRATITUDE AS A SUPERCHARGER

Gratitude is like a magic wand that amplifies everything it touches. When you're working on manifesting something, don't just focus on what you want—focus on what you already have that you're grateful for. This creates a powerful vibration of abundance that draws even more good things into your life.

A great way to use this trick is to keep a gratitude journal where you write down things you're thankful for each day. But here's the twist: include things you're grateful for that haven't happened yet, as if they already have. For example, if you're manifesting a new car, write, "I'm so grateful for my new car and how smoothly it drives." By expressing gratitude in advance, you're reinforcing your belief that it's on its way to you.

Another way to supercharge your gratitude is by turning it into a daily ritual. Take a few moments each morning or evening to close your eyes and mentally list everything you're thankful for. Let the feeling of gratitude fill your heart and radiate outwards. This positive energy helps clear any blocks and opens the door for more blessings to flow into your life.

55

CREATE A VISION BOARD

This trick is a classic but with good reason—it works! A vision board is a visual representation of your goals and desires. It's like a collage of your dreams, where you gather images, words, and symbols that represent what you want to manifest.

Creating a vision board is simple and fun. You can cut out pictures from magazines, print out images from the internet, or even draw your own. Arrange them on a board or poster and place it somewhere you'll see every day. Each time you look at your vision board, take a moment to visualise yourself living that reality and feel the emotions that come with it.

The beauty of a vision board is that it keeps your goals front and centre, reminding you daily of what you're working towards. It's a powerful tool for keeping your mind focused on your desires and reinforcing your belief that they're possible.

THE "LETTING GO" TRICK

This might sound counterintuitive, but one of the most powerful manifestation tricks is learning to let go. Once you've set your intention, visualised it, and taken action, it's important to release any attachment to how and when it will happen.

Letting go doesn't mean giving up on your desires—it means trusting that the universe will bring them to you in the best possible way and at the right time. Sometimes, our ideas of how things should unfold can limit us. By letting go, you're allowing the universe to work its magic and bring you what you want, or something even better.

When you find yourself worrying or stressing about your manifestation, gently remind yourself to let go and trust the process. Focus on living your life with joy and gratitude, knowing that what's meant for you will come. This relaxed, open attitude helps you stay in alignment with your desires and allows them to flow into your life more easily.

GRATITUDE
Vibez

MAGIC IN THE MAKING

Manifestation isn't about waving a wand and instantly getting everything you want. It's about aligning your thoughts, emotions, and actions with your desires and trusting that the universe will respond in kind. These manifestation magic tricks are tools to help you stay in that alignment, to keep your energy positive and focused, and to make the journey as joyful as the destination.

So, start using these tricks today and see how they can enhance your manifesting process. Remember, the real magic isn't just in getting what you want—it's in becoming the person who naturally attracts those things into your life. With these tricks up your sleeve, you'll be well on your way to manifesting the life of your dreams.

Enjoy the magic!

GRATITUDE IS YOUR PERSONAL RESET BUTTON—PRESS IT WHENEVER DOUBT, FEAR, OR STRESS TRIES TO TAKE OVER

Clearing the Vibe Blockers: Say Bye-Bye to Energy Drains

CHAPTER 6

What's Blocking Your Shine?
Let's Goooooooo...

Imagine you're a bright, shining light—full of potential, positivity, and the power to attract all the good things life has to offer. But sometimes, that light can feel dimmed, like there's something holding you back from being your brightest, most vibrant self. If you've ever felt stuck, like your dreams are just out of reach or your energy is off, there's a good chance that something is blocking your shine.

So, what's blocking your shine? Let's explore some of the common culprits that might be getting in the way of you living your best life and how you can clear them out to let your light shine bright again.

Self-Doubt and Negative Self-Talk

One of the biggest blocks to your shine is self-doubt. You know that little voice in your head that says, "You're not good enough," "You can't do this," or "Why even bother?" That's self-doubt talking, and it's like a cloud that covers up your light. When you listen to this voice, it can make you feel small, powerless, and stuck.

Negative self-talk goes hand in hand with self-doubt. It's the habit of criticising yourself, focusing on your flaws, and expecting the worst. These thoughts are like fog—blurring your vision and making it hard to see your true potential.

But here's the good news: self-doubt and negative self-talk are just thoughts, and thoughts can be changed. Start by becoming aware of these thoughts when they pop up. When you catch yourself thinking, "I can't," try flipping it around to, "I can, and I will." Replace negative thoughts with positive affirmations, like "I am capable," "I deserve good things," or "I am enough." The more you practice positive self-talk, the clearer and brighter your shine will become.

Fear of Failure

Fear of failure is another common block that can keep you from shining. It's the worry that if you try something new, you might not succeed, and that fear can be paralysing. It can stop you from taking risks, going after your dreams, or even trying in the first place.

But here's the thing about failure: it's not the enemy. In fact, failure is often a necessary part of growth and success. Every time you fail, you learn something valuable that brings you one step closer to your goal. When you let go of the fear of failure and embrace it as a learning opportunity, you free yourself to take chances, experiment, and discover new possibilities.

To start overcoming the fear of failure, remind yourself that no one succeeds without a few stumbles along the way. Every great achievement comes with its fair share of setbacks. The key is to keep moving forward, even when things don't go as planned. Celebrate your efforts, no matter the outcome, and give yourself credit for having the courage to try. With each step, you'll build confidence, and your shine will grow stronger.

Comparison Trap

We've all been there—scrolling through social media, seeing other people's highlight reels, and feeling like we're falling short. The comparison trap is a sneaky block that can dim your shine by making you feel like you're not measuring up. When you compare yourself to others, it's easy to forget about your own unique strengths and accomplishments.

But the truth is, everyone's journey is different. Just because someone else is shining in their own way doesn't mean your light is any less bright. You have your own path, your own timeline, and your own special gifts to offer the world.

To break free from the comparison trap, focus on your own progress and celebrate your own wins, no matter how small. Instead of comparing yourself to others, use their success as inspiration and a reminder that if they can do it, so can you. Remember, the only person you should be comparing yourself to is the person you were yesterday. Keep striving to be your best self, and let your unique light shine.

Limiting Beliefs

Limiting beliefs are those deep-seated ideas you hold about yourself and the world that keep you from reaching your full potential. They might sound like, "I'm not smart enough," "Success is for other people, not me," or "I'll never have enough money." These beliefs act like invisible barriers, preventing you from stepping into your power and shining your brightest.

The tricky thing about limiting beliefs is that they often operate under the surface, so you might not even realize they're there. But once you identify them, you can start to challenge and change them. Ask yourself, "Is this belief really true?" "Where did it come from?" and "What would my life be like if I didn't believe this?"

Replace limiting beliefs with empowering ones. For example, if you've been telling yourself, "I'm not smart enough," try replacing it with, "I am capable of learning and growing." If you believe "Success is for other people," shift it to, "Success is available to me, too." The more you affirm these new, positive beliefs, the more they'll take root, and the brighter your light will shine.

Success is available to ME NOW!

ENERGY DRAINS

ARE THERE PEOPLE IN YOUR LIFE WHO CONSTANTLY BRING YOU DOWN OR DRAIN YOUR ENERGY?

Sometimes, what's blocking your shine isn't just mental or emotional—it's physical. Energy drains are things in your life that sap your energy and leave you feeling exhausted, unmotivated, and stuck. These can include cluttered spaces, toxic relationships, unhealthy habits, or even just a lack of self-care.

When your energy is low, it's hard to shine. That's why it's important to identify what's draining your energy and take steps to clear it out. Start by decluttering your physical space—get rid of things that no longer serve you and create an environment that feels peaceful and uplifting.

Next, take a look at your relationships. Are there people in your life who constantly bring you down or drain your energy? If so, it might be time to set boundaries or even let go of those connections.

Finally, prioritise self-care. Make time for activities that recharge you, whether it's getting enough sleep, eating nourishing foods, spending time in nature, or doing something you love. When you take care of your energy, you'll feel more vibrant, and your shine will naturally return.

Feel more vibrant

VIBE DETOX
Clear out toxins...

SHINE ON

Once you've identified and cleared out the blocks that have been dimming your light, you'll be amazed at how much more you can shine. Remember, your light is unique, and the world needs you to be your brightest self. When you let go of self-doubt, fear, comparison, limiting beliefs, and energy drains, you create space for your true potential to come through.

So, what's been blocking your shine? Take a moment to reflect, and then take action to clear those blocks out of your life. You deserve to live fully, to shine brightly, and to share your gifts with the world.

Don't let anything hold you back—your time to shine is now!

VIBE DETOX

Just like your body needs a detox every now and then to clear out toxins and reset, your energy, or vibe, sometimes needs a little cleansing too. Life can get busy, stressful, and overwhelming, and all those negative vibes can start to build up, leaving you feeling drained, stuck, or just out of sync with the good things you want to attract. That's where a Vibe Detox comes in—an energetic cleanse to help you shake off the bad vibes and get back to feeling your best, most positive self.

A Vibe Detox is all about clearing out the negative energy that's weighing you down and replacing it with positive, uplifting vibez. It's like hitting the reset button for your spirit, helping you realign with your true self and the high-frequency energy that attracts abundance, joy, and peace. Ready to get started? Let's dive into some simple and effective ways to give your vibe a much-needed detox.

DECLUTTER YOUR SPACE, DECLUTTER YOUR MIND

Your physical environment plays a huge role in how you feel. When your space is cluttered and chaotic, it can create a sense of overwhelm and stress, which can drag your vibe down. That's why one of the first steps in a Vibe Detox is to clear out your physical space.

Start by decluttering the areas where you spend the most time—your bedroom, living room, or workspace. Get rid of anything that doesn't serve you, whether it's old clothes, unused gadgets, or paperwork that's piled up. As you clear out the clutter, imagine that you're also clearing out the mental and emotional clutter that's been bogging you down. You'll be amazed at how much lighter and more energised you feel when your space is clean and organised.

And don't forget to freshen up your space with some positive energy boosters. Open the windows to let in fresh air, light a candle, or add some plants or crystals to bring in good vibes. Your environment should feel like a sanctuary—a place that supports your well-being and helps you stay in a positive, high-vibe state.

UNPLUG AND RECHARGE

In today's digital world, we're constantly bombarded with information, notifications, and social media updates. While technology has its benefits, it can also be a major source of stress and negativity, especially if you're always plugged in. That's why part of your Vibe Detox should include a digital detox.

Take some time to unplug from your devices—whether it's for a few hours, a full day, or even a weekend. Use this time to reconnect with yourself and the real world around you. Go for a walk in nature, read a book, meditate, or spend quality time with loved ones. Notice how much more peaceful and present you feel when you're not constantly checking your phone or scrolling through social media.

While you're at it, consider doing a little social media cleanse. Unfollow or mute accounts that bring you down or make you feel less than. Instead, fill your feed with positive, uplifting content that inspires you and supports your goals. Remember, what you consume digitally can have a big impact on your vibe, so choose wisely!

SHAKE OFF THE STRESS

Stress is one of the biggest culprits when it comes to blocking your vibe. It can weigh you down, sap your energy, and make it hard to stay positive and focused. That's why it's so important to find ways to shake off stress as part of your Vibe Detox.

Exercise is one of the best ways to release stress and boost your vibe. Whether it's going for a run, hitting the gym, practicing yoga, or dancing around your living room, moving your body helps to clear out stagnant energy and release endorphins—those feel-good chemicals that naturally lift your mood.

Breathwork is another powerful tool for detoxing your vibe. When you're stressed, your breath tends to become shallow and quick, which only adds to your anxiety. By practicing deep, mindful breathing, you can calm your nervous system and bring your energy back into balance. Try taking a few minutes each day to practice deep belly breathing, where you inhale deeply through your nose, fill your lungs, and exhale slowly through your mouth. This simple practice can make a big difference in how you feel.

Clear out what drains you, and let gratitude flood your life with fresh energy

RELEASE NEGATIVE EMOTIONS

Holding onto negative emotions like anger, resentment, or sadness can seriously block your shine. These emotions are like heavy baggage that weighs you down and keeps you stuck in a low-vibe state. Part of your Vibe Detox is about letting go of these emotions so you can move forward with a lighter, brighter energy.

One way to release negative emotions is through journaling. Write down what you're feeling without holding back—get it all out on paper. Sometimes, just acknowledging and expressing your emotions can be incredibly healing. After you've written everything down, you might even want to do a little ritual where you tear up the paper or burn it (safely, of course) as a symbolic way of letting go.

Another powerful way to release negative emotions is through forgiveness. This doesn't mean you have to condone someone's behaviour or forget what happened, but it does mean choosing to release the hold that anger or resentment has over you. Forgiving others and yourself allows you to free up space in your heart and mind for more positive, loving energy.

NOURISH YOUR BODY AND SOUL

A Vibe Detox isn't just about clearing out the negative—it's also about filling yourself up with positive, nourishing energy. That means taking care of your body and soul in a way that supports your overall well-being.

Start by nourishing your body with healthy, whole foods that make you feel good from the inside out. Eating a balanced diet rich in fruits, vegetables, whole grains, and lean proteins can boost your energy levels and keep your vibe high. And don't forget to stay hydrated—drink plenty of water to keep your body and mind functioning at their best.

For your soul, focus on activities that bring you joy and help you connect with your true self. This could be anything from meditation and yoga to creative hobbies like painting, writing, or playing music. Spend time in nature, practice gratitude, and surround yourself with people who uplift and inspire you. The more you do things that light you up, the more your vibe will naturally rise.

EMBRACE POSITIVITY

Finally, one of the most important parts of a Vibe Detox is embracing positivity in all its forms. This means not only thinking positive thoughts but also speaking positively, acting with kindness, and choosing to focus on the good in every situation.

One way to do this is by practicing positive affirmations. These are simple, powerful statements that you repeat to yourself to reinforce a positive mindset. Examples might include, "I am worthy of love and success," "Good things are coming my way," or "I am surrounded by positive energy." The more you affirm these positive beliefs, the more they'll become your reality.

Another way to embrace positivity is by spreading it to others. Acts of kindness, no matter how small, can have a huge impact on your vibe. Whether it's complimenting someone, holding the door open, or just offering a smile, these small gestures create a ripple effect of positivity that benefits everyone, including you.

SHINE BRIGHT

A Vibe Detox is all about clearing out the negative energy that's been holding you back and filling yourself up with positivity, joy, and love. By taking the time to detox your vibe, you're giving yourself the gift of a fresh start—a chance to reconnect with your true self and let your light shine bright.

So, what are you waiting for? Start your Vibe Detox today and watch as your energy, mood, and life begin to transform. You deserve to feel amazing, and with a clear, high-vibe energy, there's nothing you can't achieve. Shine on!

FORGIVE AND FLY FREE

Imagine carrying around a heavy backpack filled with rocks. Each rock represents a grudge, a hurt, or a resentment that you've been holding onto. Over time, the weight of that backpack starts to slow you down, making it harder to move forward and enjoy life. Now, imagine what it would feel like to set that backpack down, to let go of those heavy rocks, and to finally feel light, free, and able to soar. That's what forgiveness can do for you—it's the key to releasing the weight of the past and opening yourself up to a brighter, more joyful future.

Forgiveness isn't always easy, but it's one of the most powerful things you can do for yourself. When you choose to forgive, you're not condoning the hurt or forgetting what happened. Instead, you're making a conscious decision to let go of the pain and resentment that's been holding you back. You're choosing to free yourself from the emotional burden and allow healing to take place. Forgiveness is like cutting the ties that keep you tethered to the past so you can spread your wings and fly free.

THE HEALING POWER OF FORGIVENESS

Holding onto anger, resentment, or bitterness doesn't just affect your mood—it can also take a toll on your mental and physical health. Studies have shown that harbouring negative emotions can lead to increased stress, anxiety, and even physical ailments like high blood pressure and a weakened immune system. On the other hand, forgiveness has been linked to numerous health benefits, including lower stress levels, improved relationships, and a greater sense of well-being.

Forgiveness is a gift you give to yourself. It's about reclaiming your peace of mind and taking back your power. When you forgive, you're no longer allowing someone else's actions to control your emotions or your life. Instead, you're choosing to focus on your own healing and happiness. It's a powerful act of self-love that allows you to move forward with a lighter heart and a clearer mind.

FORGIVING OTHERS

When it comes to forgiving others, it's important to remember that forgiveness is a process, not a one-time event. It's okay if you're not ready to forgive right away—sometimes, it takes time to process your emotions and come to terms with what happened. The first step is simply to acknowledge the pain and recognise that holding onto it isn't serving you.

Start by reflecting on the situation and the emotions you're feeling. Allow yourself to feel whatever comes up without judgement. Once you've acknowledged your feelings, ask yourself if you're ready to let go of the resentment and move on. If you are, try to see the situation from a different perspective. What might the other person have been going through? What can you learn from this experience? Sometimes, understanding the other person's perspective can help soften your heart and make forgiveness easier.

If you're struggling to forgive, try writing a letter to the person who hurt you. You don't have to send it—this is just for you. In the letter, express your feelings honestly and openly. Let it all out. Then, end the letter by stating your intention to forgive. You might say something like, "I choose to forgive you because I deserve peace," or "I release this pain and free myself from the past." When you're finished, you can choose to keep the letter as a reminder of your strength, or you can tear it up or burn it as a symbolic act of letting go.

Forgiveness frees you, and gratitude helps you soar

FORGIVING YOURSELF

Sometimes, the hardest person to forgive is yourself. We all make mistakes, and it's easy to get caught up in self-blame and guilt. But holding onto those negative feelings only keeps you stuck in the past. Forgiving yourself is about recognising that you're human, that you're learning and growing, and that you deserve compassion just as much as anyone else.

Start by acknowledging what you're holding onto. Maybe it's something you said, something you did, or even something you didn't do. Whatever it is, take a moment to reflect on the situation and how it's affecting you. Then, ask yourself, "Would I judge a friend as harshly as I'm judging myself?" Chances are, you wouldn't. So why not offer yourself the same kindness and understanding?

To forgive yourself, it can be helpful to practice self-compassion. This means treating yourself with the same care and gentleness you would offer a loved one. Remind yourself that it's okay to make mistakes and that each mistake is an opportunity to learn and grow. You might even try saying out loud, "I forgive myself," and really let those words sink in. Forgiving yourself is an act of self-care that allows you to move forward with confidence and a renewed sense of self-worth.

THE FREEDOM OF FORGIVENESS

When you choose to forgive, you're choosing freedom. You're freeing yourself from the chains of the past and opening the door to a future filled with possibility. Forgiveness doesn't mean you have to forget what happened or even reconcile with the person who hurt you. It simply means that you're no longer letting that pain define you or dictate your life.

Imagine what your life would look like without the weight of resentment or guilt. How much lighter would you feel? How much more joy and peace could you experience? Forgiveness allows you to reclaim your power and live your life on your own terms. It's about choosing to focus on the good, to embrace love and compassion, and to create a future that's free from the shadows of the past.

FLYING FREE

As you embark on your journey of forgiveness, remember that it's a process. Be patient with yourself and take it one step at a time. Some days, forgiveness may feel easy, while other days, it might feel like a struggle. That's okay. What's important is that you're making the effort to let go and move forward.

Forgiveness is your ticket to freedom. It's the key to unlocking your full potential and living a life that's true to who you are. So, let go of the heavy backpack, release the rocks of resentment and guilt, and feel the lightness that comes with forgiving and flying free. Your wings are ready—it's time to soar.

FORGIVENESS IS FREEDOM

HIGH VIBES AREN'T AN ACCIDENT—THEY'RE A CHOICE. FUEL YOUR ENERGY WITH GRATITUDE AND WATCH YOUR WORLD TRANSFORM

Gratitude Love Fest: Supercharge Your Relationships

CHAPTER 7

GRATITUDE IN ACTION

More than enough

Gratitude isn't just something you feel inside—it's also something you can share with the people around you. When you express gratitude in your relationships, you create a ripple effect of positivity that can transform those connections into deeper, more meaningful, and love-filled adventures. It's amazing how a simple "thank you" or a heartfelt expression of appreciation can strengthen bonds, brighten someone's day, and even bring more joy and harmony into your life.

Let's explore how putting gratitude into action can make your relationships richer and more fulfilling.

The Magic of Saying "Thank You"
Sometimes, the simplest things have the biggest impact. A sincere "thank you" can do wonders for your relationships. Whether it's thanking your partner for making dinner, appreciating a friend for their support, or acknowledging a colleague for their help, these small moments of gratitude can strengthen your connections and make others feel valued.

When you make it a habit to express gratitude regularly, it shows the people in your life that you don't take them for granted. It lets them know that their efforts, big or small, are noticed and appreciated. Over time, this creates a positive feedback loop—when people feel appreciated, they're more likely to continue being kind, supportive, and loving, which in turn gives you more reasons to be grateful.

The next time someone does something kind or thoughtful for you, take a moment to express your gratitude. Look them in the eyes, smile, and say "thank you" from the heart. It might seem like a small gesture, but it can make a big difference in how connected you feel to the people in your life.

Turning Everyday Moments into Opportunities for Gratitude
One of the beautiful things about gratitude is that it doesn't have to be reserved for big, special occasions. In fact, some of the most powerful expressions of gratitude happen in the everyday moments that we often overlook.

For example, if your partner makes you a cup of coffee in the morning, take a moment to express your appreciation. If your friend listens to you vent about a tough day, let them know how much it means to you. Even in moments of conflict or disagreement, finding something to be grateful for—like the opportunity to communicate openly or the fact that you care enough to work through it—can help defuse tension and bring you closer together.

These everyday acts of gratitude might seem small, but they add up over time. They create an atmosphere of mutual respect, love, and appreciation that strengthens your relationships and makes them more resilient to challenges.

Gratitude as a Bridge in Tough Times
Every relationship faces challenges, whether it's a misunderstanding, a disagreement, or a rough patch where things just don't feel as connected as they used to.

During these times, gratitude can act as a bridge that helps you navigate through the difficulties and find your way back to each other.

When tensions are high or you're feeling disconnected, take a step back and focus on what you're grateful for in the relationship. Maybe it's the history you share, the good times you've had, or the qualities you admire in the other person. By focusing on the positives, you can shift your perspective from what's wrong to what's right, which can make it easier to approach the situation with empathy and understanding.

Expressing gratitude during tough times can also remind the other person that you value the relationship and are committed to working through the challenges together. It's a way of saying, "I see the good in you, and I appreciate what we have," even when things aren't perfect. This can soften the edges of conflict and create a space for healing and reconnection.

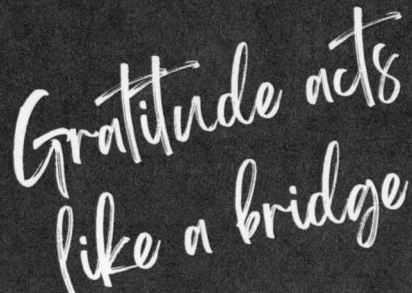

CREATING LOVE-FILLED ADVENTURES THROUGH GRATITUDE

When you make gratitude a regular part of your relationships, you're not just maintaining the status quo—you're actively creating opportunities for deeper connection and shared joy. Gratitude has a way of turning ordinary moments into love-filled adventures, where every interaction becomes a chance to strengthen your bond and build lasting memories.

Imagine planning a day with your partner, friend, or family member that's centred around gratitude. You could start by expressing what you appreciate about each other, then spend the day doing activities that you both enjoy, making sure to acknowledge and savour the good moments as they happen. Whether it's a hike in nature, a fun day at an amusement park, or simply a cosy day at home, infusing the experience with gratitude can make it feel even more special.

You can also create traditions of gratitude in your relationships. For example, you might start a ritual of sharing what you're grateful for at the dinner table, writing each other appreciation notes, or celebrating "gratitude anniversaries" where you reflect on the positive moments you've shared over the past year. These practices not only keep the gratitude flowing but also deepen your connection and make your relationships more meaningful.

GRATITUDE: THE KEY TO LASTING LOVE AND CONNECTION

At the heart of every strong, healthy relationship is a foundation of mutual respect, love, and appreciation. Gratitude is like the glue that holds all of these elements together, helping you navigate the ups and downs of life while keeping your relationships strong and vibrant.

By putting gratitude into action, you're not only enriching your own life but also making the people around you feel valued, loved, and appreciated. It's a simple yet powerful way to build deeper connections, create lasting memories, and turn your relationships into the love-filled adventures they're meant to be.

So, the next time you're with someone you care about, take a moment to express your gratitude. Notice the impact it has on both of you, and watch as your relationships blossom into something even more beautiful. With gratitude at the centre, your relationships can truly become the adventures of a lifetime.

THE GRATITUDE LOVE LANGUAGE

We've all heard of the five love languages—the different ways people express and receive love, such as through words of affirmation, acts of service, quality time, physical touch, and gifts. But there's another love language that often goes unspoken yet holds incredible power to deepen our connections and strengthen our relationships: the Gratitude Love Language.

Gratitude, when practiced regularly and sincerely, can communicate love, appreciation, and respect in ways that go beyond words. It's a language that everyone understands, and it has the ability to create an atmosphere of positivity and warmth in all of your connections. Whether it's with your partner, family, friends, or even colleagues, learning to speak the Gratitude Love Language can transform the way you relate to others and bring more love and harmony into your life.

EXPRESSING GRATITUDE: MORE THAN JUST WORDS

When we think about expressing gratitude, our minds often go straight to saying "thank you." And while verbal expressions of gratitude are important, the Gratitude Love Language goes much deeper than that. It's about showing appreciation in ways that resonate with the people around you, making them feel truly seen, valued, and loved.

For some, this might mean going out of your way to do something thoughtful—like surprising your partner with their favorite treat, helping a friend move, or taking on a task for a coworker who's overwhelmed. For others, it might be about spending quality time together, giving them your full attention, or simply being there when they need someone to talk to. The key is to understand what makes the other person feel appreciated and to express your gratitude in a way that aligns with that.

In many cases, actions speak louder than words. When you show gratitude through your behavior—whether it's by being patient, offering support, or simply smiling warmly—you're sending a powerful message that says, "I care about you, and I'm grateful to have you in my life." This nonverbal communication can strengthen bonds and create a sense of closeness that words alone might not achieve.

THE POWER OF SMALL GESTURES

In the Gratitude Love Language, small gestures can have a big impact. It's often the little things that make the biggest difference in our relationships—those moments of thoughtfulness that show someone you're paying attention and that you care.

For example, if your partner is always the one who takes care of a certain chore, surprise them by doing it yourself one day. If a friend mentioned they were having a tough week, send them a text to check in and let them know you're thinking of them. If a coworker stayed late to help with a project, bring them their favourite coffee the next morning as a thank you.

These small acts of gratitude might seem insignificant, but they add up over time and can create a strong foundation of trust, appreciation, and love. They show the people in your life that you notice the little things they do and that you value their presence. In return, you'll likely find that these gestures are reciprocated, creating a cycle of gratitude that enhances all of your relationships.

GRATITUDE AS A RELATIONSHIP BOOSTER

One of the most powerful aspects of the Gratitude Love Language is its ability to boost the overall health and happiness of your relationships. When gratitude is a regular part of your interactions, it creates a positive atmosphere where both parties feel appreciated and valued. This can lead to stronger emotional bonds, increased satisfaction, and a greater sense of connection.

Research has shown that couples who regularly express gratitude to each other tend to have stronger, more resilient relationships. Gratitude helps partners feel more satisfied with their relationship, more committed to each other, and more likely to work through challenges together. It's a simple yet effective way to keep the love alive and thriving.

But it's not just romantic relationships that benefit from the Gratitude Love Language. Friendships, family connections, and even professional relationships can all be enhanced by the regular practice of gratitude. When people feel appreciated, they're more likely to respond with kindness, cooperation, and a desire to reciprocate. This creates a positive feedback loop that makes all of your connections more enjoyable and fulfilling.

LISTENING WITH GRATITUDE

Another powerful way to speak the Gratitude Love Language is through active listening. When you truly listen to someone, you're showing them that you value their thoughts, feelings, and experiences. This kind of attention is a form of gratitude in itself—it's saying, "I'm grateful for your presence, and I care about what you have to say." Active listening involves being fully present in the moment, making eye contact, and responding thoughtfully to what the other person is sharing. It means setting aside distractions and really tuning in to their words and emotions. By listening with gratitude, you create a safe space for open communication and deepen your connection with the other person.

The next time someone shares something with you, whether it's a story about their day or a more serious concern, practice listening with gratitude. Acknowledge their feelings, ask questions to show your interest, and offer support if needed. This kind of listening can make the other person feel truly heard and appreciated, which strengthens your relationship and fosters mutual respect and understanding.

CULTIVATING A GRATITUDE MINDSET

To truly master the Gratitude Love Language, it's important to cultivate a mindset of gratitude that extends to all areas of your life. This means making a conscious effort to focus on the positives, appreciate the people around you, and express your gratitude regularly.

Start by making gratitude a daily habit. Each day, take a moment to reflect on what you're grateful for, and think about how you can express that gratitude to others. It could be as simple as sending a text to a friend, leaving a note for your partner, or giving a sincere compliment to a coworker. The more you practice gratitude, the more natural it will become, and the more it will infuse your relationships with positivity and love.

Remember, the Gratitude Love Language isn't about grand gestures or extravagant expressions—it's about the consistent, everyday acts of appreciation that show the people in your life that they matter. By making gratitude a central part of your interactions, you can create deeper, more meaningful connections that are built on a foundation of love, respect, and mutual appreciation.

THE GRATITUDE LOVE LANGUAGE
Love speaks louder when wrapped in gratitude

LOVE IN ACTION

The Gratitude Love Language is a powerful way to communicate love and appreciation without needing to say much at all. It's about letting your actions speak for themselves, showing the people in your life that you value them through thoughtful gestures, active listening, and a consistent practice of gratitude.

When you embrace the Gratitude Love Language, you're not just improving your relationships—you're also enhancing your own sense of well-being and happiness. Gratitude has the power to transform how you see the world and how you connect with others, making your life richer, fuller, and more love-filled.

So, start putting gratitude into action today. Notice the impact it has on your relationships, and enjoy the deeper connections and love-filled adventures that follow. With the Gratitude Love Language as part of your life, your relationships will shine brighter than ever before.

HEALING WITH HEART
Inner love...

Relationships aren't always smooth sailing. Even in the closest connections, there can be moments of friction—misunderstandings, disagreements, or hurt feelings that create distance between you and someone you care about. But here's the good news: gratitude has the power to heal, to bridge the gap, and to turn even the trickiest relationships into ones filled with understanding, respect, and, yes, even friendship.

Healing with heart means approaching those difficult relationships with compassion and a willingness to see the good in the other person, no matter how challenging the situation may be. It's about using gratitude as a tool to patch up the cracks, mend the wounds, and transform friction into a foundation for a stronger, more positive connection.

START WITH YOURSELF: CULTIVATING INNER GRATITUDE

Before you can use gratitude to heal a relationship, it's important to start with yourself. Healing begins within, and that means cultivating a sense of inner gratitude—gratitude for your own strengths, for the lessons you've learned, and for the growth that challenges have brought you.

Take some time to reflect on what you appreciate about yourself and your journey. Maybe it's your resilience in the face of adversity, your ability to learn from past mistakes, or simply your desire to improve your relationships. By focusing on what's good within you, you'll be better equipped to extend that same grace and appreciation to others.

Once you've centered yourself in gratitude, you can begin to approach the tricky relationship from a place of strength and positivity. This mindset shift is key to healing, as it allows you to see the situation not as a battle to be won, but as an opportunity to grow and reconnect.

FINDING THE SILVER LININGS

In every challenging relationship, there's something to be grateful for, even if it's not immediately obvious. Finding these silver linings can help you shift your perspective and open the door to healing.

Start by asking yourself, "What can I learn from this situation?" or "How has this person contributed to my life, even in a difficult way?" For example, a challenging relationship might have taught you patience, resilience, or the importance of setting boundaries. Or perhaps it has helped you become more empathetic or understanding of different perspectives.

By focusing on the lessons and growth that have come from the relationship, you can begin to feel a sense of gratitude for the person, even if the relationship has been difficult. This doesn't mean ignoring the pain or pretending everything is fine; it's about recognising the value that has come from the experience and using that as a foundation for healing.

EXPRESSING GRATITUDE, EVEN WHEN IT'S HARD

One of the most powerful ways to heal a tricky relationship is to express gratitude directly to the other person. This can be tough, especially if there's been a lot of hurt or misunderstanding. But expressing gratitude, even in small ways, can be a transformative act that softens the tension and creates a space for reconciliation.

You don't have to dive into deep, emotional conversations right away. Start with something simple. Acknowledge the positive qualities you see in the other person, or thank them for something they've done that you appreciate. For example, you might say, "I know we've had our differences, but I appreciate how you've always been there when I needed help," or "Thank you for your honesty—I know it's not always easy to speak your truth."

These small acts of gratitude can open the door to more meaningful conversations and help rebuild trust. When someone feels appreciated, they're more likely to let down their guard and respond with kindness and understanding. Gratitude can break down walls and pave the way for healing and renewal.

THE POWER OF LISTENING WITH GRATITUDE

Sometimes, healing a relationship is less about what you say and more about how you listen. When there's friction, it's easy to get caught up in defending your own point of view or trying to prove that you're right. But healing with heart means putting aside your need to be right and focusing on truly understanding the other person.

This is where listening with gratitude comes in. When you listen with gratitude, you're not just hearing the words—they're saying; you're also appreciating the effort they're making to communicate with you. You're acknowledging their perspective, even if it's different from your own, and you're showing that you value their feelings and experiences.

To practice listening with gratitude, approach the conversation with an open heart and mind. Instead of planning your response while the other person is speaking, focus fully on what they're saying. Reflect back what you've heard to ensure you understand, and express appreciation for their willingness to share with you. For example, you might say, "I appreciate you taking the time to explain how you're feeling," or "Thank you for being honest with me—I know this isn't easy."

By listening with gratitude, you create a safe space for open and honest communication, which is essential for healing any relationship.

Gratitude is the gentle touch that heals even the deepest wounds

GRATITUDE AS A DAILY PRACTICE

Healing tricky relationships doesn't happen overnight—it's a process that requires patience, commitment, and a daily practice of gratitude. By consistently focusing on the positives, expressing appreciation, and listening with an open heart, you can gradually transform even the most challenging connections.

Make gratitude a regular part of your interactions with the person. Look for opportunities to acknowledge the good, to say "thank you," and to show that you value their presence in your life. Over time, these small acts of gratitude will begin to add up, creating a foundation of trust, respect, and mutual understanding.
And remember, healing with heart isn't about ignoring the challenges or pretending everything is perfect. It's about choosing to focus on what's good and using that as a starting point for growth and connection. It's about recognising that every relationship has its ups and downs, but with gratitude, even the tough times can be a source of strength and transformation.

FROM FRICTION TO FRIENDSHIP

As you practice gratitude in your tricky relationships, you may find that the friction begins to fade, replaced by a deeper sense of understanding and connection. What was once a source of stress or tension can become a meaningful friendship, built on a foundation of mutual respect and appreciation.

Healing with heart takes time, effort, and a willingness to see the good in others, even when it's hard. But the rewards are well worth it. By using gratitude to patch up those cracks and mend the wounds, you can turn friction into friendship and create relationships that are stronger, healthier, and more fulfilling than ever before.

So, the next time you're faced with a challenging relationship, remember the power of gratitude. Approach the situation with an open heart, express your appreciation, and watch as the healing begins. With gratitude, even the trickiest relationships can be transformed into love-filled adventures.

Gratitude grows prosperity

WHEN LIFE GETS TOUGH, GRATITUDE IS YOUR ANCHOR. IT WON'T ERASE THE STORM, BUT IT WILL AND WATCH YOUR KEEP YOU STEADY

Gratitude Glow-Up: How Thankfulness Heals and Thrills

CHAPTER 8

Feel-Good Gratitude
Boost your health...

Gratitude isn't just a feel-good emotion; it's also a powerful tool for boosting your overall health and well-being. When you make gratitude a regular part of your life, the benefits go far beyond simply feeling happier or more positive. From glowing skin to a healthier heart, gratitude has a surprising number of physical and mental health benefits that can leave you looking and feeling your best. Let's dive into the ways that gratitude can supercharge your health and help you thrive from the inside out.

The Gratitude Glow: Radiant Skin from Within

Ever heard the saying that happiness is the best makeup? Well, gratitude might just be the secret ingredient to that natural glow you've been chasing. When you practice gratitude regularly, it can have a positive impact on your skin—yes, your skin!

Here's how it works: Stress is one of the biggest culprits behind skin issues like acne, dullness, and premature aging. When you're stressed, your body produces more cortisol, a hormone that can trigger inflammation and lead to breakouts, dryness, and other skin problems. But when you focus on gratitude, it helps reduce stress levels, which in turn can lower cortisol production. The result? Clearer, more radiant skin that reflects the positivity you're cultivating within.

Additionally, gratitude promotes better sleep, and we all know that getting enough rest is essential for maintaining healthy skin. When you sleep, your body goes into repair mode, healing and rejuvenating your skin cells. By practicing gratitude, especially before bed, you're more likely to enjoy a restful night's sleep, which means you wake up with that refreshed, well-rested glow.

A Happy Heart: Gratitude's Impact on Cardiovascular Health

Your heart isn't just a metaphorical symbol of love and joy—it's also a key player in your physical health. And guess what? Gratitude can help keep your heart healthy and happy.

Studies have shown that people who regularly practice gratitude have lower blood pressure and a reduced risk of heart disease. When you focus on what you're grateful for, it helps calm the nervous system and reduces the body's stress response. This leads to lower blood pressure and a slower heart rate, both of which are important for maintaining cardiovascular health.

Gratitude also promotes positive emotions, which are linked to better heart health. When you feel grateful, you're more likely to experience emotions like joy, contentment, and love. These positive feelings can help protect your heart by reducing inflammation and improving overall cardiovascular function.

So, by making gratitude a daily habit, you're not just lifting your spirits—you're also giving your heart a much-needed boost, helping it stay strong and healthy for years to come.

Strengthening Your Immune System with Gratitude

Another surprising benefit of gratitude is its ability to strengthen your immune system. When you're grateful, your body is better equipped to fight off illness and keep you feeling your best.

Here's why: Gratitude helps reduce stress, and when stress levels are low, your immune system functions more effectively. Chronic stress can weaken your immune response, making you more susceptible to infections and illnesses. But by practicing gratitude, you're helping to create a more balanced, resilient immune system that's ready to take on whatever comes your way.

In addition, gratitude is linked to better sleep, as we mentioned earlier, and getting enough sleep is crucial for immune function. When you're well-rested, your body is better able to repair and regenerate, which includes strengthening your immune defences.

So, if you want to keep the sniffles at bay and stay healthy all year round, start by cultivating an attitude of gratitude. Your immune system will thank you!

> **Gratitude isn't just for your heart—it's a glow-up for your whole body.**

Gratitude and Mental Health: A Natural Mood Booster

Of course, we can't talk about the health benefits of gratitude without mentioning its powerful impact on mental health. Gratitude is one of the most effective natural mood boosters out there, helping to reduce symptoms of anxiety and depression while promoting overall emotional well-being.

When you focus on what you're grateful for, it shifts your attention away from negative thoughts and worries. This simple shift in perspective can help reduce feelings of anxiety and stress, making it easier to stay calm and centred, even in challenging situations.

Gratitude also increases the production of dopamine and serotonin—two neurotransmitters that play a key role in regulating mood. When these "feel-good" chemicals are flowing, you're more likely to experience happiness, contentment, and a sense of overall well-being.

Regular gratitude practice has even been shown to improve self-esteem and reduce feelings of envy or resentment. When you're focused on what you have rather than what you lack, you're less likely to compare yourself to others or feel dissatisfied with your life. This can lead to greater emotional resilience and a more positive outlook on life.

HOW TO INCORPORATE GRATITUDE INTO YOUR HEALTH ROUTINE

Now that you know how powerful gratitude can be for your health, you might be wondering how to make it a regular part of your routine. The good news is, it's easier than you might think!

Start by setting aside a few minutes each day to reflect on what you're grateful for. You can do this in the morning to start your day on a positive note or in the evening to wind down before bed. Consider keeping a gratitude journal where you jot down three things you're thankful for each day. This simple practice can have a big impact on your mood and overall well-being.

You can also practice gratitude on the go by taking a moment to appreciate the little things throughout your day—a beautiful sunset, a kind gesture from a stranger, or the comfort of your favourite chair. The more you focus on these moments of gratitude, the more you'll start to notice them, creating a positive cycle of appreciation and well-being.

Another way to boost your health with gratitude is to express it to others. Whether it's thanking someone for their help, sending a note of appreciation, or simply telling a loved one how much they mean to you, expressing gratitude can strengthen your relationships and create a sense of connection and support.

GLOW FROM THE INSIDE OUT

Gratitude is more than just a nice feeling—it's a powerful tool for enhancing your health and well-being in ways you might not have imagined. From glowing skin to a happy heart, a stronger immune system to a more balanced mind, the benefits of gratitude are truly profound.

So why not start your own gratitude practice today? It doesn't take much—just a few moments of reflection each day can make a world of difference. As you cultivate gratitude, you'll begin to notice not only how it improves your mood and outlook on life but also how it helps you look and feel your absolute best.

Remember, the secret to a healthy, happy life is often found in the simplest things. And gratitude, with all its surprising health benefits, might just be the best medicine of all.

THE GRATITUDE SPA DAY

Imagine a day dedicated entirely to nurturing your body, mind, and soul—a day where you combine the powerful energy of gratitude with holistic wellness practices to create the ultimate glow-up. Welcome to your Gratitude Spa Day, a luxurious experience designed to leave you feeling refreshed, revitalised, and deeply connected to yourself. This isn't just any spa day; it's a day where every moment is infused with gratitude, turning simple self-care rituals into powerful acts of self-love and transformation.

Ready to treat yourself? Let's explore how you can create your own Gratitude Spa Day, complete with holistic practices that will leave you glowing from the inside out.

SETTING THE STAGE

Creating a Sacred Space

Before you dive into your Gratitude Spa Day, it's important to create an environment that feels peaceful, soothing, and sacred. Your space should be a sanctuary—a place where you can fully relax and focus on your well-being. Here's how to set the stage:

Declutter & Cleanse

Start by tidying up the area where you'll be spending your spa day. A clean, organised space helps create a sense of calm and clarity. Once you've decluttered, consider cleansing the energy of the room with sage, incense, or essential oils. This simple act can help clear out any lingering negative vibes and create a fresh, inviting atmosphere.

Set the Mood

Soft lighting, candles, and calming music can transform your space into a tranquil oasis. Choose scents that make you feel relaxed and happy—lavender, eucalyptus, and rose are all great options. If you have a diffuser, add a few drops of your favourite essential oil blend to fill the room with a soothing aroma.

Gather Your Tools

Think about what you'll need for your spa day—plush towels, a cosy robe, your favourite skincare products, a journal, and perhaps some herbal tea or infused water. Having everything within reach will help you stay in the flow of your self-care rituals without any interruptions.

With your space set and ready, you're all set to begin your Gratitude Spa Day.

MORNING RITUAL: GRATITUDE MEDITATION AND MINDFUL STRETCHING

Start your Gratitude Spa Day with a gentle morning ritual that awakens your body and mind while grounding you in gratitude. Begin with a gratitude meditation to centre yourself and set the tone for the day:

Gratitude Meditation
Find a comfortable seat, close your eyes, and take a few deep breaths. As you breathe in, imagine filling your body with calm, peaceful energy. As you exhale, release any tension or stress. Now, bring to mind three things you're grateful for. These could be anything from the love of a family member to the warmth of the sun on your skin. Allow yourself to fully feel the gratitude in your heart, and let it expand throughout your entire being. Spend a few minutes soaking in this feeling, allowing it to uplift and energise you.

Mindful Stretching
After your meditation, gently wake up your body with some mindful stretching. Focus on slow, deliberate movements that feel good and help you connect with your body. As you stretch, continue to focus on what you're grateful for—express gratitude for your body's strength, flexibility, and the ability to move. This practice not only helps to release tension but also deepens your connection to your body.

MID-MORNING GLOW: NOURISHING SKIN AND SOUL

Next, it's time to pamper your skin with a nourishing treatment that's infused with gratitude. This is your chance to indulge in a luxurious skincare ritual that not only leaves your skin glowing but also uplifts your spirit.

Gratitude Facial
Begin with a gentle cleanse to remove any impurities. As you wash your face, imagine washing away any negative thoughts or worries, leaving you with a clean slate for the day. Follow with a face mask that suits your skin type—whether it's a hydrating mask, a purifying clay, or a brightening sheet mask. While the mask works its magic, take a moment to thank your skin for everything it does to protect and support you. Finish with a soothing facial massage using a jade roller or your hands, applying your favourite serum or moisturiser. As you massage your skin, visualise gratitude flowing from your heart to your face, enhancing your natural glow.

Hydration and Reflection

After your facial, hydrate your body with a tall glass of infused water—add slices of cucumber, lemon, or berries for a refreshing twist. As you sip, take a few minutes to journal about what you're grateful for in your life right now. Reflect on the blessings, big and small, that make your life rich and meaningful. This act of reflection helps to reinforce your gratitude practice and keeps your heart open throughout the day.

MIDDAY RECHARGE
GRATITUDE-INFUSED NOURISHMENT

As the day progresses, it's time to nourish your body from the inside out with a mindful, gratitude-infused meal. Eating with gratitude not only enhances your enjoyment of food but also supports your overall well-being.

Mindful Eating

Prepare a meal that's both nourishing and delicious, focusing on whole, vibrant foods that make you feel good. As you cook, express gratitude for the ingredients you're using—the fresh vegetables, the flavorful herbs, the wholesome grains. Consider the journey each ingredient has taken to reach your kitchen, from the earth to your plate, and thank everyone involved in bringing this nourishment to you.

Gratitude Meal

When your meal is ready, take a moment to appreciate its beauty, aroma, and the nourishment it provides. Before you eat, pause to say a few words of gratitude for the food, for your body, and for the opportunity to enjoy this meal. As you eat, savour each bite, paying attention to the flavours and textures. Eating mindfully and with gratitude can enhance your digestion, boost your mood, and leave you feeling truly satisfied.

AFTERNOON BLISS
SOOTHING BODY RITUALS

After lunch, it's time to indulge in some soothing body rituals that help you relax, release tension, and deepen your sense of gratitude.

Gratitude Bath

Run a warm bath and add some Epsom salts, essential oils, or a bath bomb to create a luxurious soak. As you sink into the water, feel the warmth envelop you like a comforting hug. Close your eyes and take a few deep breaths, letting the water wash away any lingering stress. As you soak, mentally list the things you're grateful for—your health, your loved ones, the simple pleasures of life. Let each thought of gratitude fill you with peace and contentment.

Self-Massage

After your bath, treat yourself to a self-massage using your favourite body oil or lotion. Start at your feet and work your way up, taking your time to really feel the sensations of your hands on your skin. As you massage, thank each part of your body for the role it plays in your life—your legs for carrying you, your arms for embracing others, your heart for beating strong. This ritual not only relaxes your muscles but also deepens your appreciation for your body.

EVENING WIND-DOWN GRATITUDE FOR A PEACEFUL MIND

As your Gratitude Spa Day comes to a close, it's important to wind down with rituals that promote inner peace and prepare you for a restful night's sleep.

Gratitude Yoga

Engage in a gentle yoga practice focused on relaxation and gratitude. Choose poses that help you release tension, such as child's pose, forward folds, and gentle twists. As you move through each pose, focus on your breath and mentally express gratitude for your body's ability to stretch and move. End your practice with a few minutes in savasana (corpse pose), allowing yourself to fully relax and absorb the benefits of your day.

Evening Reflection

Before bed, take a few moments to reflect on your Gratitude Spa Day. What did you enjoy most? What are you feeling most grateful for right now? Write down your thoughts in a journal, or simply sit quietly and meditate on them. This reflection helps to anchor the positive energy you've cultivated throughout the day and sets the stage for a peaceful, restorative sleep.

SWEET DREAMS AND A LASTING GLOW

As you drift off to sleep, feel the warmth of gratitude in your heart. Know that you've spent the day nurturing yourself in the most holistic way possible—caring for your body, mind, and soul with the healing power of gratitude. The effects of your Gratitude Spa Day will linger, leaving you with a lasting glow, both inside and out.

Remember, you don't need a special occasion to treat yourself to a Gratitude Spa Day. Anytime you feel the need to recharge, reconnect with yourself, or simply indulge in some self-love, you can create this experience. The combination of gratitude and wellness is a powerful one, capable of transforming not just your appearance, but your entire outlook on life.

So go ahead, pamper yourself with gratitude, and watch as your life begins to glow with positivity, health, and joy. You deserve it!

GRATITUDE + HEALTH HACKS

Incorporating gratitude into your daily routine isn't just about feeling good—it's also about maintaining high-vibration health for both your body and mind. When you combine gratitude with some simple health hacks, you create a powerful synergy that can boost your energy, improve your mood, and enhance your overall well-being. The best part? These gratitude-infused health hacks are fun, easy to do, and can fit seamlessly into your everyday life. Ready to level up your health with the power of gratitude? Let's dive in!

MORNING GRATITUDE SMOOTHIE: NOURISH YOUR BODY AND SOUL

Kickstart your day with a gratitude smoothie—a delicious and nourishing way to fuel your body while setting a positive tone for the day. Here's how to do it:

Gather Your Ingredients
Choose your favourite smoothie ingredients—think fresh fruits, leafy greens, a scoop of protein powder, and a splash of almond milk or coconut water. As you prepare each ingredient, take a moment to express gratitude for its nourishment. For example, thank the banana for its energy-boosting potassium or the spinach for its rich iron content.

Blend with Intention
As you blend your smoothie, infuse it with positive energy. Visualise your body absorbing all the nutrients and imagine how they'll help you feel vibrant and energised throughout the day. This simple act of mindfulness turns an ordinary breakfast into a powerful gratitude practice.

Savour with Appreciation
When your smoothie is ready, take a moment to appreciate its colours, flavours, and the nourishment it provides. Sip slowly, savouring each taste, and let yourself feel grateful for the health benefits it's bringing to your body.

GRATITUDE WALKS: BOOST YOUR MOOD AND GET MOVING

Walking is one of the simplest and most effective ways to improve your physical and mental health. But when you add a dose of gratitude to your daily stroll, it becomes even more powerful. Here's how to make your walks a gratitude-infused experience:

Set a Gratitude Intention
Before you start your walk, set an intention to focus on gratitude. Decide that during your walk, you'll look for things to be grateful for—whether it's the beauty of nature, the feeling of the sun on your skin, or the simple pleasure of moving your body.

Walk with Awareness
As you walk, pay attention to your surroundings. Notice the colours of the leaves, the sound of birds, and the smell of fresh air. With each step, think of something you're grateful for. It could be as simple as being able to take this walk, the strength in your legs, or the peacefulness of the moment.

Express Gratitude
If you pass by other people, give them a smile or a friendly nod, silently thanking them for sharing the path with you. If you walk past a beautiful tree or a blooming flower, take a moment to appreciate it. This practice not only lifts your spirits but also creates a ripple of positivity in your environment.

Gratitude Journaling
for Mental Clarity...

Gratitude journaling is a powerful way to clear your mind, reduce stress, and boost your mental health. It helps you focus on the positives in your life, which can lead to greater emotional resilience and a more balanced state of mind. Here's a simple way to incorporate gratitude journaling into your daily routine:

Pick Your Time
Choose a time of day that works best for you—whether it's first thing in the morning, during your lunch break, or before bed. Consistency is key, so try to journal at the same time each day.

Write with Intention
Start by writing down three things you're grateful for. These can be big or small—anything from a kind word from a friend to the comfort of your home. As you write, focus on the feelings of gratitude and let them fill your heart.

Reflect and Connect
After writing, take a moment to reflect on what you've written. How does it make you feel? How has gratitude shifted your perspective? This reflection helps deepen your practice and reinforces the positive effects on your mental health.

Gratitude Breathing
Calm Your Mind and Center Yourself

Gratitude breathing is a simple yet effective technique to calm your mind, reduce stress, and bring yourself into the present moment. It's a great way to reset during a busy day or to wind down in the evening. Here's how to practice gratitude breathing:

Find a Quiet Space
Sit comfortably in a quiet space where you won't be disturbed. Close your eyes and take a few deep breaths to settle in.

Breathe in Gratitude
As you inhale, imagine breathing in feelings of gratitude. Picture a warm, golden light filling your lungs, representing all the things you're thankful for. Let this light spread throughout your body, bringing a sense of peace and contentment.

Exhale Tension
As you exhale, release any tension, stress, or negative thoughts. Imagine the air leaving your body, carrying away anything that's weighing you down. Continue this pattern for a few minutes, allowing yourself to relax and centre your mind.

Gratitude Hydration
Drink to Your Health

Staying hydrated is crucial for your health, but did you know you can turn drinking water into a gratitude practice? It's a simple hack that not only keeps you hydrated but also keeps your vibe high throughout the day. Here's how to practice gratitude hydration:

Bless Your Water
Before you take a sip, take a moment to appreciate the water you're about to drink. Thank it for hydrating your body, cleansing your system, and keeping you energised. This small ritual can turn an ordinary glass of water into a powerful act of self-care.

Drink Mindfully
As you drink, focus on the sensation of the water quenching your thirst and refreshing your body. Visualise it nourishing your cells and giving you the energy you need to thrive. This mindfulness practice helps you stay present and connected to your body's needs.

Stay Grateful
Throughout the day, continue to express gratitude for the water you drink. Whether you're refilling your water bottle or grabbing a quick sip, let each drink be a reminder of the abundance in your life.

The healthiest lifestyle is one where gratitude fuels the mind, body, and spirit

GRATITUDE AFFIRMATIONS

ENERGISE YOUR BODY AND MIND

Affirmations are powerful statements that can shift your mindset and keep your energy high. When combined with gratitude, they become even more effective. Here's how to use gratitude affirmations to energise your body and mind:

Create Your Affirmations
Write down a few gratitude-based affirmations that resonate with you. For example: "I am grateful for my strong, healthy body," "I am thankful for the abundance of energy I have today," or "I appreciate the balance and peace in my life."

Repeat with Intention
Repeat these affirmations to yourself throughout the day, especially during moments when you need a boost of energy or positivity. You can say them silently in your mind, out loud, or write them down in your journal.

Feel the Gratitude
As you repeat your affirmations, take a moment to truly feel the gratitude in your heart. Let the positive emotions fill you up and elevate your vibration. This practice not only energises you but also keeps you focused on the good things in your life.

Feel more gratitude

GRATITUDE SLEEP RITUAL REST AND RECHARGE

A good night's sleep is essential for maintaining high-vibration health, and a gratitude-infused sleep ritual can help you rest more deeply and wake up feeling refreshed. Here's how to create a gratitude sleep ritual:

Wind Down with Gratitude
As you prepare for bed, take a few minutes to reflect on your day. What went well? What are you grateful for? Let go of any worries or stress and focus on the positive moments.

Gratitude Nightcap
Write down three things you're thankful for on a notepad or in a journal by your bed. This simple act helps clear your mind and sets a positive tone for your sleep.

Drift Off with Peace
As you close your eyes, take a few deep breaths and repeat a gratitude affirmation, such as "I am grateful for this day and the peaceful sleep ahead." Let these words be the last thoughts you have as you drift off to sleep.

HIGH-VIBRATION HEALTH, ONE GRATEFUL STEP AT A TIME

By combining gratitude with these simple health hacks, you're setting yourself up for a life filled with high-vibration health. The more you integrate gratitude into your daily routine, the more you'll notice its positive effects on your body and mind. Whether it's through a morning smoothie, a mindful walk, or a peaceful sleep ritual, gratitude has the power to elevate every aspect of your health and well-being.

Remember, the journey to high-vibration health doesn't have to be complicated. It's about making small, consistent changes that align with your intention to live a healthy, joyful, and fulfilling life. With gratitude as your guide, you'll find that these health hacks not only boost your energy and mood but also help you create a life that truly shines from the inside out. So go ahead—embrace these simple, fun practices and let gratitude be the key to your ultimate glow-up!

Hydration and Reflection

After your facial, hydrate your body with a tall glass of infused water—add slices of cucumber, lemon, or berries for a refreshing twist. As you sip, take a few minutes to journal about what you're grateful for in your life right now. Reflect on the blessings, big and small, that make your life rich and meaningful. This act of reflection helps to reinforce your gratitude practice and keeps your heart open throughout the day.

MIDDAY RECHARGE
GRATITUDE-INFUSED NOURISHMENT

As the day progresses, it's time to nourish your body from the inside out with a mindful, gratitude-infused meal. Eating with gratitude not only enhances your enjoyment of food but also supports your overall well-being.

Mindful Eating

Prepare a meal that's both nourishing and delicious, focusing on whole, vibrant foods that make you feel good. As you cook, express gratitude for the ingredients you're using—the fresh vegetables, the flavorful herbs, the wholesome grains. Consider the journey each ingredient has taken to reach your kitchen, from the earth to your plate, and thank everyone involved in bringing this nourishment to you.

Gratitude Meal

When your meal is ready, take a moment to appreciate its beauty, aroma, and the nourishment it provides. Before you eat, pause to say a few words of gratitude for the food, for your body, and for the opportunity to enjoy this meal. As you eat, savour each bite, paying attention to the flavours and textures. Eating mindfully and with gratitude can enhance your digestion, boost your mood, and leave you feeling truly satisfied.

AFTERNOON BLISS
SOOTHING BODY RITUALS

After lunch, it's time to indulge in some soothing body rituals that help you relax, release tension, and deepen your sense of gratitude.

Gratitude Bath

Run a warm bath and add some Epsom salts, essential oils, or a bath bomb to create a luxurious soak. As you sink into the water, feel the warmth envelop you like a comforting hug. Close your eyes and take a few deep breaths, letting the water wash away any lingering stress. As you soak, mentally list the things you're grateful for—your health, your loved ones, the simple pleasures of life. Let each thought of gratitude fill you with peace and contentment.

SHINE BRIGHT

A Vibe Detox is all about clearing out the negative energy that's been holding you back and filling yourself up with positivity, joy, and love. By taking the time to detox your vibe, you're giving yourself the gift of a fresh start—a chance to reconnect with your true self and let your light shine bright.

So, what are you waiting for? Start your Vibe Detox today and watch as your energy, mood, and life begin to transform. You deserve to feel amazing, and with a clear, high-vibe energy, there's nothing you can't achieve. Shine on!

FORGIVE AND FLY FREE

Imagine carrying around a heavy backpack filled with rocks. Each rock represents a grudge, a hurt, or a resentment that you've been holding onto. Over time, the weight of that backpack starts to slow you down, making it harder to move forward and enjoy life. Now, imagine what it would feel like to set that backpack down, to let go of those heavy rocks, and to finally feel light, free, and able to soar. That's what forgiveness can do for you—it's the key to releasing the weight of the past and opening yourself up to a brighter, more joyful future.

Forgiveness isn't always easy, but it's one of the most powerful things you can do for yourself. When you choose to forgive, you're not condoning the hurt or forgetting what happened. Instead, you're making a conscious decision to let go of the pain and resentment that's been holding you back. You're choosing to free yourself from the emotional burden and allow healing to take place. Forgiveness is like cutting the ties that keep you tethered to the past so you can spread your wings and fly free.

THE HEALING POWER OF FORGIVENESS

Holding onto anger, resentment, or bitterness doesn't just affect your mood—it can also take a toll on your mental and physical health. Studies have shown that harbouring negative emotions can lead to increased stress, anxiety, and even physical ailments like high blood pressure and a weakened immune system. On the other hand, forgiveness has been linked to numerous health benefits, including lower stress levels, improved relationships, and a greater sense of well-being.

Forgiveness is a gift you give to yourself. It's about reclaiming your peace of mind and taking back your power. When you forgive, you're no longer allowing someone else's actions to control your emotions or your life. Instead, you're choosing to focus on your own healing and happiness. It's a powerful act of self-love that allows you to move forward with a lighter heart and a clearer mind.

FORGIVING OTHERS

When it comes to forgiving others, it's important to remember that forgiveness is a process, not a one-time event. It's okay if you're not ready to forgive right away—sometimes, it takes time to process your emotions and come to terms with what happened. The first step is simply to acknowledge the pain and recognise that holding onto it isn't serving you.

Start by reflecting on the situation and the emotions you're feeling. Allow yourself to feel whatever comes up without judgement. Once you've acknowledged your feelings, ask yourself if you're ready to let go of the resentment and move on. If you are, try to see the situation from a different perspective. What might the other person have been going through? What can you learn from this experience? Sometimes, understanding the other person's perspective can help soften your heart and make forgiveness easier.

If you're struggling to forgive, try writing a letter to the person who hurt you. You don't have to send it—this is just for you. In the letter, express your feelings honestly and openly. Let it all out. Then, end the letter by stating your intention to forgive. You might say something like, "I choose to forgive you because I deserve peace," or "I release this pain and free myself from the past." When you're finished, you can choose to keep the letter as a reminder of your strength, or you can tear it up or burn it as a symbolic act of letting go.

Forgiveness frees you, and gratitude helps you soar

FORGIVING YOURSELF

Sometimes, the hardest person to forgive is yourself. We all make mistakes, and it's easy to get caught up in self-blame and guilt. But holding onto those negative feelings only keeps you stuck in the past. Forgiving yourself is about recognising that you're human, that you're learning and growing, and that you deserve compassion just as much as anyone else.

Start by acknowledging what you're holding onto. Maybe it's something you said, something you did, or even something you didn't do. Whatever it is, take a moment to reflect on the situation and how it's affecting you. Then, ask yourself, "Would I judge a friend as harshly as I'm judging myself?" Chances are, you wouldn't. So why not offer yourself the same kindness and understanding?

To forgive yourself, it can be helpful to practice self-compassion. This means treating yourself with the same care and gentleness you would offer a loved one. Remind yourself that it's okay to make mistakes and that each mistake is an opportunity to learn and grow. You might even try saying out loud, "I forgive myself," and really let those words sink in. Forgiving yourself is an act of self-care that allows you to move forward with confidence and a renewed sense of self-worth.

THE SECRET TO LIVING YOUR DREAM LIFE? ACT LIKE YOU ALREADY HAVE IT, AND BE GRATEFUL EVERY STEP OF THE WAY

Gratitude Genie: Wish, Believe, Receive

CHAPTER 9

Setting Grateful Intentions
What Are Grateful Intentions?

We all have dreams and goals that we hope to achieve—whether it's landing that dream job, building meaningful relationships, improving our health, or simply living a more fulfilling life. But what if there was a way to supercharge those dreams and make them even more likely to come true? Enter the concept of setting grateful intentions—a powerful practice that combines the clarity of intention-setting with the high-vibration energy of gratitude.

When you set intentions powered by gratitude, you're not just wishing for something to happen; you're aligning yourself with the energy that can help make it a reality. This practice helps you stay focused, motivated, and positive as you work towards your goals, making the journey just as fulfilling as the destination. Ready to learn how to set grateful intentions that can turn your dreams into reality? Let's get started!

What Are Grateful Intentions?

At its core, an intention is a clear and specific statement about what you want to create, achieve, or experience in your life. It's different from a goal in that it focuses more on the journey than the destination—an intention is about how you want to feel, act, and live as you move towards your dreams.

Gratitude, on the other hand, is the practice of appreciating the good things in your life, both big and small. When you combine gratitude with intention-setting, you create what's known as a grateful intention. A grateful intention is a statement of what you want to achieve, infused with the energy of appreciation for what you already have. This powerful combination not only clarifies your desires but also attracts more positivity and abundance into your life.

Why Grateful Intentions Work?

Grateful intentions work because they tap into two powerful forces: the clarity of intention-setting and the magnetic energy of gratitude. When you're clear about what you want and genuinely grateful for the blessings you already have, you create a positive energy field around your intentions. This energy not only helps you stay focused and motivated but also attracts opportunities, resources, and people that can help you achieve your goals.

Moreover, setting grateful intentions shifts your mindset from lack to abundance. Instead of focusing on what you don't have or what's missing from your life, you're focusing on what's already good and how you can build on that. This mindset shift helps you approach your goals with a sense of confidence, optimism, and trust in the process.

How to Set Grateful Intentions

Setting grateful intentions is a simple yet powerful practice that you can incorporate into your daily routine. Here's how to do it:

Get Clear on Your Intentions

Start by reflecting on what you truly want to create, achieve, or experience in your life. Take some time to think about your dreams and goals—whether they're related to your career, relationships, health, personal growth, or any other area of your life. Be specific about what you want, but also think about how you want to feel as you work towards these goals.

Infuse Your Intentions with Gratitude

Once you're clear on your intentions, take a moment to appreciate where you are right now. What are you grateful for in this moment? How have your past experiences, both positive and challenging, prepared you for this journey? By acknowledging the good in your life, you create a strong foundation of gratitude that supports your intentions.

For example, if your intention is to find a fulfilling job, you might say, "I am grateful for the skills and experiences that have brought me to this point, and I intend to find a job that aligns with my passions and values." This statement not only sets a clear intention but also honours the journey that's led you here.

Write Down Your Grateful Intentions

Writing your intentions down helps to solidify them in your mind and make them feel more real. Use a journal, a piece of paper, or even a note on your phone—whatever works best for you. As you write, focus on the feeling of gratitude and allow it to infuse your words.

You might write something like, "I am grateful for the love and support I have in my life, and I intend to deepen my relationships with those around me," or "I am thankful for my body's strength and resilience, and I intend to prioritise my health and well-being." The key is to keep your intentions clear, positive, and rooted in gratitude.

Visualise Your Intentions Coming to Life

After writing down your intentions, take a few minutes to visualise them coming to life. Close your eyes and imagine yourself living your intentions—how does it feel? What does it look like? The more vividly you can picture your desired outcome, the more powerful your intentions become. As you visualise, allow yourself to feel deep gratitude for the fulfilment of your intentions, as if they've already happened.

Take Inspired Action

Setting grateful intentions is just the first step—next, it's time to take action. Think about the steps you can take to move closer to your goals. These actions don't have to be big or dramatic; even small, consistent steps can lead to significant progress over time. As you take action, continue to focus on gratitude, both for the steps you're taking and for the opportunities that arise along the way.

Practice Patience and Trust

Manifesting your dreams takes time, and it's important to practice patience and trust in the process. Trust that your grateful intentions are working behind the scenes, even if you don't see immediate results. Keep revisiting your intentions, practicing gratitude, and taking inspired action. Remember, the journey itself is a valuable part of the experience, and every step you take brings you closer to your dreams.

DAILY PRACTICES TO SUPPORT YOUR GRATEFUL INTENTIONS

To keep your grateful intentions alive and thriving, it's helpful to incorporate some daily practices that reinforce your commitment and keep your energy high. Here are a few ideas:

MORNING INTENTION-SETTING

Start each day by setting a grateful intention for the day ahead. It could be something simple, like "I am grateful for the opportunities today will bring, and I intend to approach each task with positivity and focus." This morning ritual helps you set a positive tone for the day and keeps your intentions front and centre.

GRATITUDE CHECK-INS

Throughout the day, take a few moments to check in with yourself and express gratitude for what's going well. Whether it's a successful meeting, a kind word from a colleague, or simply the fact that you're making progress, these gratitude check-ins help you stay aligned with your intentions and keep your energy high.

EVENING REFLECTION

At the end of the day, reflect on how your intentions played out. What went well? What challenges did you face? How did gratitude help you navigate the day? Use this reflection time to reinforce your intentions and express gratitude for the progress you've made.

TURNING DREAMS INTO REALITY WITH GRATITUDE

Setting grateful intentions is a powerful practice that can help you turn your dreams into reality. By combining the clarity of intention-setting with the positive energy of gratitude, you create a strong foundation for achieving your goals and living the life you desire.

Remember, the key to successful intention-setting is consistency and trust. Keep your intentions clear, focus on gratitude, and take inspired action every day. As you do, you'll find that the path to your dreams becomes smoother, more enjoyable, and filled with unexpected blessings.

So go ahead—start setting your grateful intentions today. Watch as your dreams begin to unfold, supported by the powerful energy of gratitude, and enjoy the journey as much as the destination. With gratitude guiding your intentions, there's no limit to what you can achieve!

THE GRATITUDE GENIE FORMULA

Imagine you've just stumbled upon an ancient lamp, dusty and hidden away, waiting for the right person to find it. You give it a little rub, and out pops a magical genie, ready to grant your wishes. But here's the twist—this isn't just any genie; it's the Gratitude Genie. And instead of simply granting your wishes with a snap of the fingers, this genie has a special formula for turning your dreams into reality: gratitude.

The Gratitude Genie Formula is all about harnessing the power of gratitude to make your wishes come true. It's a fun, magical way to think about manifesting your desires, where you play an active role in creating the life you want. Ready to learn how to work with the Gratitude Genie? Let's dive into the formula and see how you can start making your wishes a reality!

STEP 1: RUB THE LAMP—GET CLEAR ON YOUR WISH

Every good wish starts with clarity. Before the Gratitude Genie can work its magic, you need to know exactly what you want. This first step is all about getting crystal clear on your desires—what do you truly want to bring into your life? Whether it's a new job, a loving relationship, better health, or more abundance, take some time to reflect on your deepest desires.

To help with this, try writing down your wish as specifically as possible. The more detailed you are, the easier it will be for the Gratitude Genie to understand what you're asking for. For example, instead of just wishing for "happiness," you might wish for "a fulfilling career that allows me to use my talents and make a positive impact." Once you've identified your wish, write it down on a piece of paper or in a journal. This act of writing helps to solidify your intention and makes your wish feel more real.

STEP 2: MAKE YOUR WISH—VISUALISE WITH GRATITUDE

Now that you've got your wish, it's time to make it official by visualising it. But this isn't just any visualisation—it's powered by gratitude. The key to the Gratitude Genie Formula is to visualise your wish as if it's already come true and to feel deep gratitude for it, right here and now.

Find a quiet place where you can sit comfortably and close your eyes. Take a few deep breaths to relax and centre yourself. Now, bring your wish to mind and imagine it in vivid detail. Picture yourself living your wish—what does it look like? How does it feel? Who is with you? The more sensory details you can include, the better.

As you visualise, allow feelings of gratitude to fill your heart. Imagine thanking the universe, the Gratitude Genie, or whatever higher power you believe in, for granting your wish. Feel the joy, the relief, and the excitement of having your wish come true. The stronger your feelings of gratitude, the more powerful your visualisation will be.

This step is all about aligning your energy with the reality you want to create. By visualising your wish with gratitude, you're sending out a signal to the universe that you're ready to receive and that you're already grateful for what's on its way.

STEP 3: LET GRATITUDE DO THE REST—TRUST AND TAKE ACTION

After you've visualised your wish with gratitude, it's time to let go and trust that the Gratitude Genie is at work. This doesn't mean sitting back and doing nothing—it means taking inspired action while trusting that the universe is aligning everything in your favour.

Think of it this way: the Gratitude Genie has set the wheels in motion, but it's up to you to keep the momentum going. Start by taking small, actionable steps toward your wish. These steps don't have to be huge—sometimes, the smallest actions can lead to the biggest results.

For example, if your wish is to find a new job, start by updating your resume, networking with people in your industry, or applying for positions that excite you. If your wish is to improve your health, begin by incorporating healthier foods into your diet, taking regular walks, or starting a new exercise routine.

As you take these actions, continue to practice gratitude. Thank the universe for the opportunities that come your way, for the progress you're making, and for the guidance you receive along the journey. This ongoing gratitude keeps your energy high, your mindset positive, and your connection with the Gratitude Genie strong.

BONUS STEP: CELEBRATE EVERY WIN—BIG OR SMALL

One of the most magical parts of working with the Gratitude Genie is celebrating every win, no matter how big or small. Each step you take, each opportunity that arises, and each bit of progress you make is worth celebrating. Why? Because celebration reinforces the positive energy you're creating and strengthens your belief that your wish is on its way.

Whenever something good happens, take a moment to acknowledge it and express gratitude. You might say, "Thank you, universe, for this progress!" or "I'm so grateful for this opportunity!" By celebrating the small wins, you're building momentum and showing the universe that you're ready for more.

And remember, sometimes the Gratitude Genie works in mysterious ways. You might find that your wish manifests in a slightly different form than you expected or that it leads you to something even better than what you originally asked for. Stay open, stay grateful, and trust that everything is unfolding perfectly.

THE MAGIC OF THE GRATITUDE GENIE FORMULA

The Gratitude Genie Formula is a fun and powerful way to turn your dreams into reality. By combining the clarity of intention-setting with the high-vibration energy of gratitude, you're not just making a wish—you're actively creating the life you want.

So, the next time you have a wish, remember the Gratitude Genie Formula: Rub the lamp by getting clear on your desire, make your wish by visualising it with gratitude, and then let gratitude do the rest by trusting the process and taking inspired action. With the Gratitude Genie on your side, there's no limit to what you can achieve.

And most importantly, enjoy the journey! The process of manifesting your dreams is meant to be fun, exciting, and filled with joy. Celebrate every step, stay grateful, and watch as your wishes start to come true, one by one. Your life is your magical adventure, and with gratitude as your guide, anything is possible.

REAL-LIFE MAGIC STORIES

There's something truly magical about hearing real-life stories of people who have used gratitude to turn their dreams into reality. These tales aren't just feel-good anecdotes—they're powerful reminders that the practice of gratitude can have profound effects on our lives. From manifesting dream careers to finding love, these stories show how gratitude can be the catalyst for incredible transformation. So, sit back and get inspired by these real-life magic stories of people who used gratitude to make their wildest dreams come true.

Sarah's Story
From Struggling Artist to Successful Entrepreneur

Sarah had always dreamed of making a living as an artist, but after years of struggling to get her work noticed, she found herself feeling discouraged and stuck. Her art wasn't selling, and she was working multiple side jobs just to make ends meet. One day, a friend introduced her to the idea of practicing gratitude to shift her mindset and attract more abundance into her life.

At first, Sarah was skeptical, but she decided to give it a try. Every morning, she started writing down three things she was grateful for in her life. Some days, it was as simple as being thankful for a hot cup of coffee or the support of her family. As she continued this practice, Sarah noticed a subtle but powerful shift in her attitude. She began to focus more on the positives in her life rather than the challenges.

One day, during her gratitude journaling, Sarah decided to set a grateful intention: "I am grateful for the opportunity to share my art with the world and make a living doing what I love." She visualised herself as a successful artist, her work admired and sought after by many.

Within weeks of setting this intention, Sarah started noticing changes. She was inspired to reach out to local galleries, and to her surprise, one of them offered to host a solo exhibition of her work. The exhibition was a huge success, with many of her pieces selling out on the first night. As word spread, Sarah's career took off, and she was able to quit her side jobs and focus entirely on her art.

Looking back, Sarah credits her success to the power of gratitude. By shifting her mindset from scarcity to abundance, she was able to attract the opportunities and success she had always dreamed of. Today, Sarah continues to practice gratitude daily, and her art career continues to flourish.

Listen to real people....

Mark's Story
Healing a Broken Heart and Finding True Love

After a painful breakup, Mark felt lost and uncertain about his future. He struggled to move on, often replaying the relationship in his mind and wondering what went wrong. One day, while searching for ways to heal, he came across an article about using gratitude to recover from heartbreak and attract new love.

Intrigued, Mark decided to give it a try. He began each day by expressing gratitude for the lessons he had learned from his past relationship, focusing on the personal growth it had brought him. He also started a daily practice of writing down things he was grateful for in his life—his health, his friends, his job, and even the simple pleasures like a good book or a walk in the park.

As Mark practiced gratitude, he noticed his heart beginning to heal. He felt lighter, more positive, and more open to the idea of love. He decided to set a grateful intention: "I am grateful for the love that is on its way to me, and I am open to receiving it." He visualised himself in a loving, healthy relationship, filled with joy and mutual respect.

A few months later, Mark met someone new at a friend's gathering. They clicked instantly, and as they got to know each other, Mark realised that this relationship felt different—healthier, more balanced, and deeply fulfilling. It wasn't long before they fell in love, and Mark knew he had found something truly special.

Today, Mark is happier than he ever thought possible, and he credits his journey to the healing power of gratitude. By focusing on the good in his life and setting an intention for love, he was able to attract a relationship that exceeded his wildest dreams.

Gratitude really heals

REAL-LIFE MAGIC STORIES

Jessica's Story
Turning Financial Struggles into Abundance

Jessica was going through a tough time financially. Despite working hard, she always seemed to be just scraping by, and the stress of money worries was taking a toll on her health and happiness. Desperate for a change, Jessica decided to try something different: practicing gratitude as a way to shift her financial situation.

Every morning, Jessica began her day by expressing gratitude for the money she did have, even if it wasn't much. She thanked the universe for her job, her home, and the ability to pay her bills, even if it was a struggle. She also set a grateful intention: "I am grateful for the financial abundance that is flowing into my life, and I trust that I am supported by the universe."

Jessica made a conscious effort to change her mindset from one of lack to one of abundance. Instead of worrying about money, she focused on being grateful for every dollar that came her way. She started visualising herself as financially secure, with enough money to not only cover her needs but also to enjoy life and share with others.

Over time, Jessica began to notice changes. She received an unexpected bonus at work, her freelance side gig started bringing in more clients, and she even found ways to save money on her monthly expenses. But the biggest shift came when she was offered a new job that paid significantly more than her current position—an opportunity that seemed to come out of nowhere.

Jessica's financial situation improved dramatically, and she no longer felt the constant stress and worry that had plagued her for so long. She continued her gratitude practice, now more convinced than ever of its power to transform her life. Today, Jessica is not only financially secure but also feels a deep sense of peace and abundance that goes beyond money.

Michael's Story
Manifesting a Dream Home

Michael had always dreamed of living in a beautiful home surrounded by nature, but it seemed like an impossible goal. His current apartment was small and cramped, and he didn't have the financial resources to buy a new place. However, after hearing about the power of gratitude, Michael decided to give it a try and see if it could help him manifest his dream home.

Listen to real people...

Every day, Michael expressed gratitude for his current living situation, even though it wasn't ideal. He thanked the universe for providing him with a roof over his head, a place to sleep, and a space to call his own. He also started visualising his dream home in detail—imagining the garden, the cosy living room, the sunlight streaming through the windows, and the sense of peace he would feel living there.

Michael set a grateful intention: "I am grateful for the perfect home that is on its way to me, and I trust that it will come at the right time." He continued to practice gratitude, even when it felt like nothing was happening.

Then, one day, a friend mentioned that a house in a nearby town was going on the market. It was exactly the kind of place Michael had been dreaming of—a charming cottage surrounded by trees, with plenty of space and a beautiful garden.

Although he initially doubted he could afford it, Michael decided to visit the house anyway, trusting in the power of his grateful intention.

To his surprise, the house was priced within his reach, and the seller was willing to negotiate. With some creative financing and a bit of luck, Michael was able to buy the house, turning his dream into a reality. Today, he lives in his dream home, feeling more connected to nature and more at peace than ever before.

Michael's story is a testament to the magic of gratitude. By focusing on what he was grateful for and visualising his dream with intention, he was able to manifest a home that exceeded his wildest expectations.

THE MAGIC OF GRATITUDE

These real-life stories show that gratitude isn't just a feel-good practice—it's a powerful tool for manifesting your dreams and creating the life you desire. Whether it's finding love, achieving financial security, or turning a creative passion into a thriving career, gratitude has the ability to shift your mindset, attract opportunities, and open doors you never thought possible.

The common thread in all these stories is that gratitude wasn't just an afterthought—it was a central part of the journey. By focusing on what they were grateful for, setting clear intentions, and taking inspired action, these individuals were able to turn their dreams into reality.

So, what's your dream? Whether it's big or small, start by practicing gratitude today. Write down what you're thankful for, set a grateful intention, and trust that the universe is working behind the scenes to bring your dreams to life. Who knows? Your story might just be the next real-life magic tale of gratitude.

THE MOMENT YOU STOP CHASING WHAT'S MISSING AND START APPRECIATING WHAT'S HERE, LIFE GIVES YOU MORE TO BE GRATEFUL FOR

CHAPTER 10

Living in the Gratitude Groove: Make It a Lifestyle

The Gratitude Lifestyle
Let's imagine...

You wake up in the morning, the first light of day filtering through your curtains, and before your feet even touch the floor, you feel a wave of gratitude wash over you. It's not just for the big things—your health, your loved ones, your home—but also for the little things, the things that often go unnoticed. The warmth of your bed, the sound of birds outside your window, the potential of a new day. This feeling isn't fleeting; it's a constant presence in your life, something that shapes how you see the world and how you respond to it. This is the essence of the Gratitude Lifestyle.

A Gratitude Lifestyle is about more than just saying "thank you" when good things happen. It's a mindset, a way of being that stays with you, even when things aren't going your way. It's about waking up every day with a heart full of appreciation, no matter what challenges or obstacles you might face. It's not about ignoring the tough times or pretending everything is perfect; instead, it's about acknowledging the difficulties while still finding reasons to be thankful. This mindset keeps you grounded, positive, and resilient, helping you navigate life's ups and downs with grace and a sense of inner peace.

The Power of a Gratitude-Fueled Morning

Imagine starting every morning by tuning into what you're grateful for. As you wake up, instead of reaching for your phone or jumping out of bed to start your day in a rush, you take a moment to breathe and reflect on the things you appreciate. You might silently thank the universe for the restful sleep you just had, the new opportunities that the day will bring, or the simple comfort of your pillow. This morning ritual sets a positive tone for the entire day, helping you approach whatever comes your way with a mindset of abundance and appreciation.

By cultivating gratitude from the moment you wake up, you're setting yourself up to face the day's challenges with a stronger, more positive attitude. You're less likely to be thrown off by minor annoyances or setbacks because your mind is already focused on the good. And when bigger challenges arise, you have a foundation of gratitude to support you, reminding you that even in the midst of difficulty, there are things to be thankful for.

Gratitude as a Constant Vibe

Living a Gratitude Lifestyle means that gratitude isn't just something you practice occasionally—it becomes a constant vibe that infuses every aspect of your life. It's like a background melody that plays no matter what's happening around you, a steady hum of appreciation that keeps you centred and connected to what truly matters.

This constant vibe of gratitude helps you stay positive and optimistic, even when things don't go as planned. It's easy to be grateful when everything is going well, but the real power of the Gratitude Lifestyle shows up when life gets tough. When you face challenges—whether it's a stressful day at work, an argument with a loved one, or a personal setback—gratitude helps you keep things in perspective. It reminds you that there is always something good to focus on, something to appreciate, even in the darkest times.

This doesn't mean you ignore or suppress negative emotions. Instead, it means that you allow yourself to feel those emotions while also holding space for gratitude. You acknowledge the difficulty of the situation, but you also look for the silver linings, the lessons, and the small blessings that can be found even in the midst of adversity. This balanced approach keeps you grounded and helps you move through challenges with greater resilience and grace.

The Resilience of a Grateful Heart

One of the most powerful aspects of the Gratitude Lifestyle is the resilience it cultivates. Life is full of ups and downs, and it's inevitable that you'll face challenges, setbacks, and disappointments along the way. But when you approach life with a heart full of gratitude, you become more resilient—better able to bounce back from difficulties and keep moving forward.

Gratitude shifts your focus from what's wrong to what's right, from what's missing to what's present. It helps you see challenges as opportunities for growth and learning, rather than as insurmountable obstacles. This shift in perspective empowers you to take action, to find solutions, and to keep going, even when things are tough.

Moreover, gratitude has a way of attracting positivity and abundance into your life. When you consistently focus on what you're thankful for, you create a positive feedback loop that draws more good things to you. You start to notice more opportunities, attract more supportive people, and experience more moments of joy and fulfilment. This doesn't mean you'll never face difficulties, but it does mean that you'll be better equipped to handle them when they arise.

Gratitude in Action
Choosing to Focus on the Good

Living a Gratitude Lifestyle is a choice—a choice to focus on the good, no matter what. It's a daily decision to seek out the positive, to appreciate the small things, and to find joy in the simple moments. It's about choosing to see life through the lens of gratitude, even when it would be easier to focus on the negative.

This doesn't mean that you ignore or deny the challenges you face. Instead, it means that you choose to balance those challenges with a focus on what's going well, what you can be thankful for, and what you can learn from the situation. This balanced approach helps you stay centered, calm, and positive, even in the face of adversity.

For example, if you're dealing with a difficult situation at work, you might choose to focus on the support you're receiving from colleagues, the skills you're developing, or the lessons you're learning. If you're going through a tough time in your personal life, you might choose to focus on the love and support of your friends and family, the strength you're discovering within yourself, or the small moments of joy that still exist, even in the midst of difficulty.

EMBRACING THE GRATITUDE LIFESTYLE

The Gratitude Lifestyle isn't about being positive all the time or ignoring the realities of life. It's about cultivating a mindset of appreciation that helps you navigate life's challenges with grace, resilience, and a sense of inner peace. It's about making gratitude a constant vibe in your life, something that you carry with you wherever you go, no matter what life throws your way.

By embracing the Gratitude Lifestyle, you're choosing to live with a heart full of appreciation, a mind focused on the good, and a spirit that's resilient and strong. You're choosing to wake up each day with a sense of gratitude, to approach life's challenges with a positive attitude, and to find joy in the simple moments.

So, are you ready to make gratitude your everyday vibe? Start today by incorporating small practices of gratitude into your daily routine. Wake up with gratitude, carry it with you throughout the day, and end your day with a reflection on the things you're thankful for. As you do, you'll find that the Gratitude Lifestyle becomes second nature, a guiding force that helps you live your best life, no matter what.

STAYING HIGH ON THE VIBE TRAIN

Life is full of highs and lows, and it's easy to let the world's challenges drag you down. But what if you could stay "high on the vibe train," keeping your frequency elevated no matter what's happening around you? Staying high-vibe isn't about ignoring the negative or pretending that everything is perfect. Instead, it's about finding creative ways to maintain your positive energy, to bounce back quickly when things go wrong, and to keep your spirit uplifted even in the face of adversity.

Here are some creative strategies to help you stay high on the vibe train, ensuring that your energy remains elevated and your outlook bright, no matter what life throws your way.

CREATE A HIGH-VIBE PLAYLIST

Music has an incredible power to influence your mood and energy. When you're feeling low, one of the quickest ways to elevate your frequency is to turn on a playlist of your favourite high-vibe songs. Choose music that makes you feel alive, joyful, and inspired—songs that make you want to dance, sing along, or simply smile.

Consider curating different playlists for different situations—one for energising your morning, another for calming your mind before bed, and one for those moments when you need a quick pick-me-up. Whenever you feel your energy dipping, hit play and let the music work its magic. You'll be amazed at how quickly a great song can shift your mood and get you back on track.

SURROUND YOURSELF WITH UPLIFTING PEOPLE

The people you spend time with can have a huge impact on your energy levels. Surround yourself with individuals who lift you up, who inspire you, and who bring positivity into your life. These are the people who make you feel good about yourself, who encourage your dreams, and who are there to support you when things get tough.

If you find yourself around negative or draining people, it's okay to set boundaries. Protect your energy by limiting your time with those who bring you down and seeking out those who help keep your vibe high. Remember, you have the power to choose who you spend your time with, and surrounding yourself with the right people can make all the difference in staying on the high-vibe train.

PRACTICE GRATITUDE IN MOTION

Gratitude is one of the most powerful tools for keeping your frequency high, but it doesn't always have to be a quiet, reflective practice. Instead, try combining gratitude with movement to supercharge its effects. This could be as simple as taking a walk and mentally listing everything you're grateful for or dancing around your living room while thinking about the good things in your life.

The combination of physical movement and gratitude not only boosts your mood but also helps to release any stagnant energy in your body, leaving you feeling more vibrant and alive. Next time you're feeling low, try taking a gratitude walk, a yoga session infused with appreciation, or even a gratitude dance party. It's a fun, active way to keep your vibe high.

CREATE A VIBE-BOOSTING ENVIRONMENT

Your environment plays a significant role in how you feel, so why not turn your space into a high-vibe haven? Start by decluttering—getting rid of items that no longer serve you can instantly lift your energy. Next, add elements that make you feel good, like plants, crystals, or artwork that inspires you. Incorporate soothing scents with candles or essential oils, and let natural light fill your space as much as possible.

Consider creating a dedicated space in your home for vibe-boosting activities. This could be a cosy corner for meditation, a bright, inspiring spot for journaling, or a room where you can play music and dance. When your environment is filled with things that make you feel happy and inspired, it's easier to stay high-vibe, even when the outside world is challenging.

EMBRACE THE POWER OF LAUGHTER

Laughter truly is the best medicine, and it's one of the quickest ways to elevate your frequency. When you laugh, your body releases endorphins—those feel-good chemicals that boost your mood and reduce stress. Make it a point to incorporate more laughter into your daily life, whether it's watching a funny movie, sharing jokes with friends, or simply finding the humour in everyday situations.

If you're feeling down, try watching a comedy special or scrolling through funny memes. You can even practice laughter yoga—a form of exercise that combines laughter with yogic breathing techniques. The idea is that even if the laughter is forced at first, it quickly becomes genuine, leaving you feeling lighter, happier, and more energised.

VISUALISE YOUR HIGH-VIBE SELF

Visualisation is a powerful tool for staying aligned with your highest frequency. Take a few moments each day to visualise your "high-vibe self"—the version of you that's confident, joyful, and living life to the fullest. Imagine how this version of you thinks, acts, and feels. Picture yourself moving through the day with ease, handling challenges with grace, and radiating positivity.

This practice helps you embody the energy you want to attract and keeps you focused on the kind of person you aspire to be. Whenever you feel your vibe slipping, close your eyes and reconnect with this high-vibe version of yourself. Let this vision guide your thoughts, actions, and decisions, helping you stay on track and aligned with your highest potential.

ENGAGE IN CREATIVE EXPRESSION

Creativity is a direct line to your soul, and engaging in creative activities is a fantastic way to keep your frequency high. Whether it's painting, writing, playing music, or even cooking, creative expression allows you to tap into your inner joy and flow state. When you're in the creative zone, you're fully present, free from worry, and connected to something greater than yourself.

Make time for creativity in your daily routine, even if it's just for a few minutes. Don't worry about the outcome—focus on the process and let your creativity flow freely. This practice not only boosts your mood but also helps you stay connected to your true self, making it easier to maintain a high frequency.

Gratitude is the magic you carry everywhere

REFRAME CHALLENGES AS OPPORTUNITIES

Staying high on the vibe train doesn't mean avoiding challenges—it means reframing them as opportunities for growth and learning. When life throws you a curveball, instead of letting it bring you down, ask yourself, "What can I learn from this?" or "How can this challenge help me grow?" By shifting your perspective, you turn obstacles into stepping stones and keep your energy focused on solutions rather than problems.

This mindset helps you maintain a high frequency even when things aren't going perfectly. It allows you to approach life with curiosity and resilience, knowing that every experience, good or bad, is an opportunity to evolve and expand.

FINAL THOUGHTS: STAY ON TRACK, STAY HIGH-VIBE

Staying high on the vibe train is all about making intentional choices that support your energy, your mood, and your overall well-being. It's about finding creative, fun ways to keep your frequency elevated, even when life tries to bring you down. Whether it's through music, creativity, laughter, or mindful practices, you have the power to stay connected to your highest self and maintain a positive outlook no matter what.

Remember, life will always have its ups and downs, but with the right tools and mindset, you can navigate those challenges while keeping your vibe high. So, hop on the vibe train, keep these strategies in your back pocket, and enjoy the journey of living your most vibrant, joyful life!

THE GRATITUDE VISION

Imagine your life as a blank canvas, waiting for you to fill it with your dreams, desires, and aspirations. Now, envision holding a paintbrush dipped in the vibrant colors of gratitude—each stroke infused with appreciation, each hue representing the blessings you already have and the ones yet to come. This is the power of the Gratitude Vision, a way of envisioning your future with gratitude at the very center, allowing you to create a life filled with joy, abundance, and fulfillment.

The Gratitude Vision isn't just a fleeting thought or a wishful daydream. It's a deliberate, conscious practice of shaping your future by focusing on what you're grateful for now and what you aspire to be grateful for in the future. When you approach your life with gratitude at the heart, you align yourself with the energy that attracts more of what you desire, turning your dreams into reality. Let's explore how you can create your own Gratitude Vision and watch the magic unfold in your life.

BEGIN WITH GRATITUDE: A FOUNDATION FOR YOUR VISION

Before you start painting the picture of your future, it's important to ground yourself in the present moment and acknowledge all the things you're grateful for right now. Gratitude is the foundation upon which your vision will be built. It's what gives your dreams substance and power, turning them from mere wishes into something tangible and achievable.

Take a moment to reflect on the blessings in your life—your health, your relationships, your accomplishments, and even the challenges that have shaped you. Write them down, or simply hold them in your heart. By starting with gratitude, you're not only appreciating what you have, but you're also setting a positive, abundant tone for the vision you're about to create.

ENVISION YOUR IDEAL FUTURE DREAM BIG WITH GRATITUDE

With gratitude as your foundation, it's time to envision your ideal future. Close your eyes and let your imagination run wild. Picture yourself living the life of your dreams—what does it look like? Where are you? Who are you with? What are you doing? Allow yourself to dream big, without limitations.

As you paint this picture in your mind, infuse it with gratitude. Imagine yourself in your dream home, waking up each day feeling grateful for the space you've created. Picture yourself in a fulfilling career, surrounded by colleagues and clients who appreciate you, and feel the gratitude for the opportunities that have led you there. Visualise yourself in vibrant health, feeling thankful for your body's strength and resilience.

The key to the Gratitude Vision is to not only see these things as possibilities but to feel the gratitude as if they've already happened. This feeling is what aligns you with the energy of your desires, making them more likely to manifest in your life.

CREATE A GRATITUDE VISION BOARD
A VISUAL REPRESENTATION OF YOUR DREAMS

One powerful way to bring your Gratitude Vision to life is by creating a vision board. A vision board is a collage of images, words, and symbols that represent the future you want to create. When you look at it, it should evoke feelings of gratitude and excitement about the life you're working towards.

To create your Gratitude Vision Board, gather magazines, print out images from the internet, or even draw your own pictures. Choose images that resonate with your dreams and desires—places you want to visit, goals you want to achieve, relationships you want to nurture, and so on. As you arrange these images on your board, take a moment to express gratitude for each one, as if it's already a part of your life.

Place your vision board somewhere you'll see it every day, like in your bedroom, office, or even as the background on your phone or computer. Each time you look at it, take a moment to feel grateful for the future you're creating. This daily practice reinforces your vision and keeps you aligned with the energy of gratitude, making it easier to manifest your dreams.

SET GRATEFUL INTENTIONS
ANCHOR YOUR VISION WITH PURPOSE

With your vision clear and your gratitude flowing, it's time to set some intentions. Grateful intentions are powerful statements that anchor your vision in reality. They're like signposts that guide you towards your desired future while keeping you grounded in the present moment.

To set your grateful intentions, think about the key areas of your life—health, career, relationships, personal growth, and so on. For each area, write a statement that reflects both your vision and your gratitude. For example:
- Health: "I am grateful for my strong, healthy body and for the energy that flows through me every day."
- Career: "I am thankful for the fulfilling work I do and for the abundance it brings into my life."
- Relationships: "I am grateful for the love and support of my family and friends, and I nurture these connections with joy."

These intentions serve as reminders of what you're working towards while also keeping you focused on the gratitude that's already present in your life.

TAKE INSPIRED ACTION
Bring Your Vision To Life...

The Gratitude Vision isn't just about dreaming—it's about taking inspired action to make those dreams a reality. Gratitude helps you stay motivated and focused, but it's the actions you take that will bring your vision to life.

Think about the steps you can take to move closer to your ideal future. They don't have to be big or overwhelming—sometimes, the smallest actions can have the greatest impact. Maybe it's reaching out to a mentor, starting a new healthy habit, or taking a class to learn a new skill. Whatever it is, approach it with gratitude and a sense of purpose.

As you take these steps, continue to express gratitude for the progress you're making, no matter how small. This keeps your energy high and your focus sharp, ensuring that you stay on track to achieve your vision.

TRUST THE PROCESS
LET GRATITUDE GUIDE YOU

One of the most important aspects of the Gratitude Vision is trust—trust in yourself, trust in the process, and trust in the timing of your dreams. There will be times when things don't go as planned, when obstacles arise, or when progress seems slow. In these moments, it's crucial to stay connected to your gratitude and trust that everything is unfolding exactly as it should.

Gratitude helps you stay patient and open, even when the path ahead isn't clear. It reminds you that every experience, whether positive or challenging, is part of your journey and brings you closer to your ultimate vision. By staying grateful and trusting the process, you allow the magic to unfold in its own time and way.

REFLECT AND CELEBRATE
ACKNOWLEDGE THE MAGIC AS IT UNFOLDS

As you work toward your Gratitude Vision, take time to reflect on the progress you've made and celebrate the milestones you've achieved. Gratitude isn't just for the big wins—it's also for the small victories and the lessons learned along the way.

Make it a habit to regularly review your vision, your intentions, and the actions you've taken. Acknowledge the magic that's already unfolding in your life, and express gratitude for it. This reflection not only keeps you motivated but also deepens your appreciation for the journey you're on.

THE POWER OF THE GRATITUDE VISION

The Gratitude Vision is a powerful tool for creating a life filled with joy, abundance, and fulfillment. By placing gratitude at the heart of your vision, you're not only focusing on what you want to achieve, but you're also appreciating what you already have. This dual focus creates a positive feedback loop that attracts more of what you desire, turning your dreams into reality.

As you continue to paint the picture of your future with gratitude, you'll find that the magic begins to unfold in unexpected and beautiful ways. Opportunities will arise, connections will be made, and you'll discover that the life you've envisioned is not only possible but already within your reach.

So, pick up your paintbrush, dip it in the vibrant colours of gratitude, and start creating your Gratitude Vision today. Watch as the magic unfolds, and enjoy the journey of turning your dreams into a reality that's even more beautiful than you imagined.

Your energy is your signal—keep it strong by fueling it with gratitude

GRATITUDE OPENS THE DOOR —ABUNDANCE WALKS IN

Your Gratitude Journey

CONCLUSION

The Gratitude Journey Ahead
One last thing...

As you take a moment to look back on your life, can you see how far you've come? The challenges you've faced, the victories you've celebrated, the lessons you've learned—all of these experiences have shaped you into the person you are today. But there's one powerful force that has been quietly guiding you along this path, helping you to grow, heal, and thrive: gratitude.

Your Gratitude Journey is more than just a series of isolated moments of thankfulness. It's a profound transformation that has touched every part of your life, elevating your spirit, strengthening your resilience, and opening your heart to the abundance that surrounds you. As you reflect on this journey, you'll realise that gratitude isn't just a practice—it's a lifelong co-pilot that will continue to steer you towards your highest potential.

Reflecting on Your Transformation
The Power of Gratitude

Think back to where you were when you first began to consciously practice gratitude. Maybe you started by keeping a gratitude journal, jotting down a few things you were thankful for each day. Or perhaps you began with small acts of appreciation, saying "thank you" more often or pausing to recognize the good in your life. At the time, these actions might have felt simple, even ordinary. But as you look back now, you can see just how extraordinary they were.

Gratitude has a way of creating a ripple effect in your life. What started as a small, intentional practice began to weave itself into the fabric of your daily routine, changing the way you see the world. You started to notice the little things—those everyday moments of joy that might have gone unnoticed before. Your perspective shifted from one of lack to one of abundance, and you found yourself focusing more on what you have rather than what you don't.

Over time, gratitude has helped you navigate life's ups and downs with greater ease. In moments of challenge, it became a lifeline—a reminder that even in the darkest times, there is something to be thankful for. It has softened your struggles, brought clarity to your decisions, and strengthened your resilience. Gratitude has taught you to see setbacks as opportunities for growth, to find silver linings in difficult situations, and to appreciate the journey, not just the destination.

Embracing Gratitude as Your Lifelong Co-Pilot

As you reflect on the incredible transformation that gratitude has brought into your life, it's clear that this practice is more than just a tool—it's a trusted companion, a co-pilot on the journey of life. Embracing gratitude as your lifelong co-pilot means recognising its power to guide you through whatever lies ahead, helping you to stay centred, positive, and aligned with your true self.

Gratitude isn't something you outgrow or move past; it's a lifelong practice that deepens and evolves as you do. As you continue on your journey, gratitude will be there to support you, reminding you to stay present, to appreciate the good, and to trust in the process. It will help you to cultivate a mindset of abundance, to attract more of what you desire, and to build stronger, more meaningful connections with the people around you.

By embracing gratitude as your co-pilot, you're choosing to live with an open heart and a positive outlook. You're committing to seeing the beauty in the world, to celebrating your successes, and to learning from your challenges. You're choosing to live a life that's rich in meaning, joy, and fulfillment— a life that's guided by the power of graitude.

Carrying Gratitude Forward
The Next Chapter of Your Journey

As you move forward on your Gratitude Journey, it's important to remember that this is just the beginning. The practice of gratitude is limitless, and there's always more to explore, learn, and experience. Every day offers a new opportunity to deepen your practice, to discover new sources of gratitude, and to let this powerful energy guide you toward your highest potential.

Consider how you can continue to cultivate gratitude in your life. Maybe it's by expanding your gratitude practice to include new rituals or by sharing your journey with others, helping them to discover the transformative power of gratitude for themselves. Perhaps it's by setting new intentions that are infused with appreciation, or by creating a vision for your future that's rooted in thankfulness for all that you've already achieved.

Whatever path you choose, know that gratitude will be there to support you every step of the way. It will help you to stay grounded during difficult times, to celebrate your successes, and to appreciate the beauty and wonder of everyday life. With gratitude as your co-pilot, you can approach the future with confidence, knowing that you have a powerful ally by your side.

Celebrating Your Journey
Acknowledge and Honor Your Growth

Before you take the next step on your journey, take a moment to celebrate how far you've come. Reflect on the growth you've experienced, the challenges you've overcome, and the blessings you've received. Acknowledge the role that gratitude has played in your transformation, and honor the commitment you've made to living a life of appreciation and abundance.

Celebrate the small wins, the big victories, and everything in between. Take pride in the fact that you've chosen to embrace gratitude, even when it wasn't easy, and that you've allowed this practice to shape your life in meaningful and positive ways. As you celebrate, feel the gratitude in your heart— gratitude for the journey, for the lessons learned, and for the incredible future that lies ahead.

THE ENDLESS JOURNEY OF GRATITUDE

Your Gratitude Journey is a lifelong adventure, one that will continue to unfold in beautiful and unexpected ways. With gratitude as your co-pilot, there are no limits to what you can achieve, experience, and enjoy. Every moment, every challenge, and every success is an opportunity to deepen your connection to gratitude and to let this powerful energy guide you towards your dreams.

As you move forward, remember that your journey is unique, and that it's okay to take it one step at a time. Trust in the process, stay open to the lessons that gratitude has to offer, and know that you are always supported. With gratitude by your side, you can navigate life's twists and turns with grace, resilience, and a heart full of appreciation.

So, take a deep breath, smile, and step confidently into the next chapter of your life. Your Gratitude Journey is far from over—in fact, it's just beginning. Embrace the adventure, let gratitude be your guide, and watch as your life continues to unfold in magical and wonderful ways.

A FINAL SPRINKLE OF MAGIC

As you reach the end of this journey, remember that you've only just begun to tap into the incredible power of gratitude. You've explored the transformative magic that comes from living with a heart full of appreciation, and you've seen how gratitude can elevate your energy, attract abundance, and help you navigate life's challenges with grace. But the best part? The journey doesn't end here—it's a lifelong adventure that keeps getting better and better.

Think of gratitude as a wave—one that you've learned to ride with skill and confidence. This wave carries you through life's ups and downs, helping you stay afloat when the waters get rough and propelling you forward towards your dreams when the tide is just right. The more you ride this wave, the more natural it becomes, until it's second nature to you, a way of being that you embody every day.

But like any wave, gratitude has its own rhythm. There will be moments when you feel like you're riding high, effortlessly gliding towards your goals, and there will be times when the wave feels more like a gentle ripple, a subtle reminder to stay present and grounded. No matter where you are on the wave, know that gratitude is always there to support you, to lift you up, and to guide you towards your most abundant life.

KEEP RIDING THE WAVE
DAILY PRACTICES FOR LASTING ABUNDANCE

To keep the magic of gratitude alive in your life, it's important to continue your daily practices—those simple yet powerful rituals that keep your gratitude flowing and your energy high. Whether it's journaling, meditation, or simply taking a moment to appreciate the small things, these practices are the foundation of your gratitude journey.

But don't stop there—keep exploring new ways to weave gratitude into your everyday life. Maybe it's through creative expression, like painting or writing, where you infuse your work with appreciation. Or perhaps it's through mindful movement, like yoga or walking, where you connect with your body and the world around you with a thankful heart. The possibilities are endless, and the more you experiment, the more you'll discover what resonates with you.

Remember, gratitude isn't just a tool for attracting abundance—it's a way of life. It's a mindset that colours your world with positivity, a lens through which you see the beauty in everything, and a force that keeps you connected to the present moment. By continuing to ride the gratitude wave, you're choosing to live with intention, to focus on what's good, and to trust that the universe has your back.

MANIFESTING YOUR MOST ABUNDANT LIFE

As you continue to ride the gratitude wave, you'll find that it naturally leads you towards a life of abundance—one where your dreams become reality, your goals are within reach, and your heart is full of joy. Gratitude opens the door to opportunities, attracts supportive people into your life, and creates a positive feedback loop that brings even more good things your way.

But abundance isn't just about material wealth or external success—it's about feeling rich in all areas of your life. It's about having meaningful relationships, good health, personal growth, and a sense of purpose. It's about waking up each day excited to see what life has in store and going to bed each night with a heart full of thanks.

When you focus on gratitude, you're not just manifesting a specific outcome—you're cultivating a life that feels abundant in every way. You're aligning yourself with the energy of abundance, which naturally attracts more of what you desire. So keep dreaming big, keep setting your intentions, and keep trusting that the wave you're riding will take you exactly where you're meant to go.

A DOSE OF MOTIVATION
STAY COMMITTED TO THE JOURNEY

There will be times when life throws you a curveball, when the challenges seem overwhelming, or when you feel like the wave has flattened out. In these moments, it's easy to lose sight of your gratitude practice, to get caught up in the stress and forget the magic that gratitude brings. But these are the times when gratitude is most important—when it has the power to pull you out of the darkness and back into the light.

When you feel your energy dip, remember that you have the tools to lift yourself back up. Take a deep breath, return to your gratitude practice, and trust that the wave will rise again. Even the smallest acts of gratitude—a simple "thank you," a quick note in your journal, or a moment of reflection—can reignite your spark and get you back on track.

Stay committed to the journey, no matter what. Gratitude is a practice, not a destination, and like any practice, it requires consistency, patience, and dedication. But the rewards are worth it—a life filled with abundance, joy, and fulfillment, where you're able to manifest your deepest desires and navigate life's challenges with grace.

A FINAL SPRINKLE OF MAGIC

As you continue on your path, take this final sprinkle of magic with you: the knowledge that gratitude is your greatest ally, your most powerful tool for creating the life you want. It's the secret sauce that turns dreams into reality, challenges into opportunities, and everyday moments into miracles.

Keep your heart open, your mind focused on the good, and your spirit aligned with gratitude. Trust that the wave you're riding will carry you to places you've never even imagined, and know that with each stroke of gratitude, you're painting a masterpiece—your most abundant, beautiful life.

So go ahead—ride that wave, embrace the magic, and watch as your life unfolds in ways that are more extraordinary than you could have ever dreamed. The journey is yours, and with gratitude as your guide, there's nothing you can't achieve. Here's to your most abundant life—may it be filled with love, joy, and endless gratitude.

Gratitude attracts miracles

TO MY DAUGHTER I LOVE YOU!

REMEMBER GRATITUDE IS THE ATTITUDE